Beyond Suez

Permission Not Granted

Meg Drummond Ross

Grosvenor House
Publishing Limited

This book is published by
Grosvenor House Publishing Ltd
Link House
140 The Broadway, Tolworth, Surrey, KT6 7HT.
www.grosvenorhousepublishing.co.uk

A CIP record for this book
is available from the British Library

ISBN 978-1-78623-103-1

About the author:

Meg Drummond Ross lived in Hong Kong for many years with her family, where she taught English as a foreign and second language to Asian students of all nationalities.

She also taught in the Hong Kong Vietnamese camps. Meg's travels began from Hong Kong in the late 1970s and early 80s, after the children left for study in the U.K.

Acknowledgements

Especial thanks go to Lucy Griffith for her invaluable help, typing skills and cover design. Thanks also to the writing groups I attended for their encouragement. Finally to Louisa Aspden, Ruth Figgest and my publisher Grosvenor House Publishing, in particular Becky Banning, for their interest and support.

Now is the season of sailing: for already
The chattering swallow is come and
The pleasant wind; the meadows
Flower and the sea tossed up with
Waves and rough blasts has sunk
To silence. Weigh thine anchors, and
Unloose thine hawsers, O mariner and
Sail with all thy canvas set.

Leonidas of Tarentum fl.274 B.C.
Greek Mythology. J.W. Mikhail
ed. (1906)

For my parents, husband, beloved daughter, sons and grandchildren.

Trip to Nagaland

SHILLONG

When I was a teenager in Scotland my mother mentioned I was born in the land of the Naga headhunters. I remember saying 'thank you very much Mother, for bringing me home safely', and promptly forgot about it. In later life I discovered I had two birth certificates: one states that I was born outside British India and the other that I am British, due to my British parents.

I had omitted to ask my mother for more information prior to her demise and my father had died earlier, but I saw from the death certificate that they had met and married in Nagaland. Now I wanted to know more and thought it was time to find out. The first certificate mentioned Shillong so I decided to start there. After various painful injections I secured an Indian visa and flew Indian Airlines to Calcutta in 1978. From there, there was a connecting flight to Bogdugra, a tiny airport in the north.

At customs I was asked for my permit. I knew nothing about a permit and handed over my passport, which was accepted. I then caught a taxi to Siliguri, a busy, bustling town, starting point for those going on to Darjeeling hill station. After a night in a hotel, I went to buy a train ticket to

Gauhati, which sits alongside the great Brahmaputra river and is the gateway to Shillong.

At the ticket counter, the man was not very helpful when I inquired of the platform.

'Up there.' He replied.

'Where?'

'There, number one up.'

'Number one up?'

End of conversation. A coolie, standing nearby, hoisted my suitcase on to his head, crooked his finger and, with a 'Memsahib', we were off. I followed his disappearing figure trying to keep my bobbing turquoise case in sight. He raced through the crowds, up steps, down steps, up again. Two uniformed officials attempted to stop me, but as my coolie was fast vanishing into the melee, I brushed past them and crossed a bridge onto a crowded platform. There were bearded Sikhs in glorious turbans, some wearing white dhotis, others in western clothes. Hundreds of passengers were milling about, some clad in only a loin cloth. Officials shouted over the hubbub, adding to the noise. I did not see any women, but I did see number three on a sign. I called my coolie's attention to this and held up one finger. He reciprocated with three. This pantomime lasted for some time before I gave in and sat down amongst the piles of cases.

The train chugged in, steaming, dirty and long, sending a billow of smoke skywards. The crowd immediately surged forward and a struggle to climb aboard ensued. I lost sight of my case. The pushing, shoving throng had no time for a single woman, so I stood back and awaited the outcome. Ten minutes later a beaming face, a crook of the finger, a 'Memsahib' and my coolie appeared to lead me to my carriage. Bless him. I thanked him with a large tip; white teeth flashing he bowed, and ran off to his next customer.

The compartment revealed four bunks, three of which had bedrolls, the fourth, a coating of thick dust. Soon, three gentlemen entered, sat down on a bunk and regarded me doubtfully. Slightly apprehensive I smiled politely, and approached the matter of a bedroll. Fortunately, English is spoken throughout India. I was informed that a bedroll was reserved with one's ticket –in advance. I must have looked crestfallen as one gentleman kindly offered me his. By this time the train had left the station. One man, probably uncomfortable at sharing a cabin with a woman and a foreigner at that, left the carriage and returned with an attendant. He explained that, as I had not reserved a bunk, there was other accommodation and he ushered me through seemingly endless carriages to a cabin occupied by two Europeans, Jack and Isobel, who were on a field trip.

Isobel was tall and willowy, fair hair cascading over her shoulders. She was a public relations lady who worked in a travel agency in Kathmandu, Nepal. Jack was a photographer, living in Nepal and making a series of wildlife films. They were on their way to Khazaranga National Park, a seven-hour taxi ride from Gauhati. We spent a pleasant journey exchanging information and sharing food. At night we stretched out on the bench seats. Sleep was impossible. The train seemed to stop at every village and town. The noise was endless: animals grunting, railway gangs working, people shouting, lights shining through the wooden shutters. Finally, we crossed the great Brahmaputra, wide and grey in the pre-dawn mist. It was 5:30 a.m. when we bade goodbye and good luck to each other (we were to meet again quite unexpectedly). When Westerners crossed paths in India they would say good luck –you never knew if you would ever arrive at your chosen destination.

The platform was crowded and I got lost looking for the exit. Finding myself on the same platform once more, a man approached asking if I required a taxi.

'I don't know. I want to go to Shillong.'

'Ah cha, you need a taxi, come.' I was to learn that this 'come' was an imperative issued by Indian men expecting an immediate response from a woman. I went. Once more my case was taken; I hoisted my rucksack on to my shoulder and we set off in the dark. We crossed a bridge on to the concourse where, along its length, dark heaps lay. I stooped to examine one and was dismayed to discover sacks in which men, women and children were sleeping.

I caught up with my case as it was being loaded into a car. I climbed into the car and waited for the driver. One hour and three passengers later, my suitcase was removed and tied to the roof. By this time I was starving. Dawn was creeping over the horizon revealing a sky suffused with a red-golden light. I left the car and sat down at a stall for tea and naan, and was joined by a large, bearded Sikh who informed me he was the fifth passenger and we could now leave. Five people climbed into the car as more luggage was tied to the roof. Gauhati is a sprawling, fair-sized town and by the time we had passed through I was perspiring in my jeans and t-shirt. The driver, the Sikh and I were squeezed into the front; a family of three sat comfortably in the back.

I soon forgot my discomfort and enjoyed the passing scenery. It was the dry season in Assam. Bullocks grazed, banana trees lined the wide roadway and gangs repaired the roads with picks and shovels. There was no other traffic, apparently because private cars were scarce. Any vehicles were lorries, government cars or old taxis. I could vouch for the old. We stopped at a village for a welcome drink and bananas. The cups were dirty and cracked so I drank from a straw while swatting at flies. The Sikh paid my bill, ignoring my protests, and I wandered through the village, stepping on discarded fruit skins. Thin dogs, their bony ribs showing, lay by the road. With my pale face, blue eyes and auburn hair, people stared but did not approach. I looked in vain for a toilet and then slipped, nonchalantly, into bushes. Emerging, I was greeted with knowing smiles, no privacy here then. There was a stall selling leaves and a reddish paste that the owner wrapped in a leaf and gestured for me to try. Game for anything, I did, spitting it out. It was betel nut, which left me with a very red tongue and teeth and caused a roar of laughter from the villagers.

We resumed our journey after the car had undergone repairs. Looking out of the window I felt a tingling sensation in my leg. I slapped and jiggled, thinking it must be a mosquito or a fly. Five minutes later another one. I looked at the Sikh. He was staring straight ahead, his hand tucked between my leg and his. I lifted my leg and drove my shoe down onto his foot. He groaned, looked at me reproachfully and removed his hand. What price bananas and tea? Six hours later, after several stops for repairs, we arrived in Shillong. Five relieved people tumbled out, exhausted, thirsty and hungry.

The driver clambered on to the roof, untied the ropes and handed down our luggage. I paid my share of the taxi, waved goodbye and stood waiting for a local taxi. After fifteen minutes a black car stopped and there was my Sikh, sitting comfortably in the back seat and offering me a lift to my hotel. With no idea where my hotel was, and with no sign of another vehicle, I reluctantly climbed in beside the chauffeur. My host immediately apologised for his previous lapse of behaviour and made up for it by telling me about the area.

Called the 'Scotland of the East', Shillong is one of India's premier hill stations. It lies approximately 1,496 meters above sea level and is the capital of what is now known as Meghalaya – an autonomous state within Assam since 1972.It is land-locked, surrounded by the verdant Khasi and Jaintia hills. Nearby is Cherapungi which (at that time) had the world's heaviest rainfall. I remembered my father had mentioned that. Meghalaya has a temperate climate, the main occupation agriculture, but with many small industrial mills. To the south and west is Bangladesh. There is fishing, hiking and golfing, river valleys and lakes. There are panthers, tigers, leopards, elephants and bears, all declining in numbers. There are deer, goats and squirrels.

We soon arrived at my hotel which resembled a large stone house. The extensive grounds housed cottages for the guests. My Sikh pressed his card into my hand with a murmured, 'in case you need help', as his driver unloaded my suitcase and quickly drove off. Hotel staff lifted my luggage and showed me to reception. My priority was a pot of tea. In the lounge the staff were pleasant and helpful, but slow. After fifteen minutes I repeated my order and was told it was coming; fifteen minutes later, it did. This was India, patience required. Sit down and relax, I admonished.

Taking my key I walked through the garden to my cottage. Inside, mosquito netting adorned the bed, doors and windows. Hmm, I had forgotten about those pesky little beasts. After a refreshing shower and change, I set off for the town and hospital, with directions from reception. Some distance later, lost and walking in circles, I turned back and, with more directions, finally located the hospital of my birth.

A notice proclaimed this as the Khasi Hills Presbyterian Hospital, formerly known as the Welsh Mission Hospital, opened in 1922. I went in search of a nurse and explained my presence. She kindly took me to the old wing where we surmised I had been born. It was a long, low building with a pitched roof and a veranda with French windows opening outwards. A lovely tropical garden gave a peaceful ambience. I thanked her, and she thanked me in return for 'coming all the way from Scotland to visit them.' I stood in the grounds trying to imagine those times. There would have been no cars to take people to hospital, but bullock carts for transport and no excellent roads, as now. How my father had worked on the great Ganges and Brahmaputra rivers; how Western families had taken to the hill stations to avoid the long, hot summers of the plains. It was romantic from a distance, but it must have been taxing at times.

I returned to the town passing stalls, shops and busy bazaars. In the background there was a sprinkling of modern flats and bungalows with red tiled roofs and I wondered fleetingly if my Sikh lived there, in an opulent house. In a park I sat on the grass in the shade of a large tree and, taking out a pack of cigarettes, lit one, lay down and closed my eyes.

I soon felt movement near me. To the side there sat a handsome young man of about twenty.

'I'm Rhaka, I would like to practise my English,' he announced in perfect English. 'I'm a student. Do you mind if I have a cigarette?' He asked, as he helped himself.

Curiosity overcame me, and I sat up. 'Help yourself.'

'What is your name? I would like to invite you for dinner.'

This was an interesting, rather sudden chat-up line. And we did chat while he took photographs. He was studying architecture and hoped to travel to Europe one day. Exhausted and hot, I declined his invitation but promised to return the next day at the same time.

I showered and changed for dinner. The dining room was a large space with wooden flooring, high ceilings and tables covered with dazzling white tablecloths. As I walked across the floor my footsteps click-clacked, echoing loudly in the almost deserted room. Two European men who were sharing a table looked up, smiled and invited me to join them. I was enjoying India; everyone was friendly.

John was travelling independently and had chanced this way. They had met in the hotel where Roland was staying, teaching at the local college. Both were biologists. John invited me to join him on his travels, but I was on a pilgrimage and so declined. We parted after a very interesting evening accompanied by a tasty, spicy dinner.

In the morning, I went to the registrar's office in town to find out if they had birth records, and whether Shillong was outside British India in the days of the Raj. The young assistant did not know so I asked about records and was informed that the registrar held the keys. He was supervising at Gandhi's election office and would not return till the next day. Disappointed, I returned to the hotel where I was almost knocked down by a chap just leaving. He apologised in English. As we chatted he asked what I was doing in India. We sat down for tea and I related my story. I had to return to Gauhati for my onward journey to Nagaland. He was an accountant, working for Gandhi, paying the salary of those officers at the election polls in the north. He was leaving shortly for Gauhati and would give me a lift. I could not believe my luck and with the thought of another taxi ride in mind, gratefully accepted. I packed my case and rucksack, paid my bill and wrote an apologetic note to Rhaka, hoping he would call at the hotel. I never had the opportunity to return to the registrar's office; maybe the answer was in Nagaland.

GAUHATI

My companion's name was Prem and his travelling companion was Lomas. While working for government they had a car and driver. Prem was tall, well built. He had deep-set black eyes and a thick moustache and was very impatient and intense. His wife and children lived in Gujarat, so he was quite far from home. His colleague, Lomas, was older, more practical, a calming influence. The driver was a potential Stirling Moss who took bends fast and furious as he sped through the night, arriving at dusk in Gauhati – much quicker than my previous tortured journey. My companions booked into a small hotel in town, after which we went for dinner to a restaurant-cum-nightclub, to enjoy many delicious, spicy dishes. Later, the driver dropped me off at the tourist lodge.

Previously called Dak bungalows, and used by government officials, these lodges are state managed and almost every town in the north has one. This one was a low storeyed building with fourteen good-sized rooms and some family rooms with bunk beds. There was a spacious bathroom, mosquito nets on the bed, a small wooden table, two chairs and a dodgy lock. In the grounds there was a large windowless bus in which three Dutch people had driven overland to explore India. We wished each other luck and moved on.

The following morning the manager asked me to register with my permit number, which of course I did not have, but promised to produce it after breakfast. Prem saved me from my predicament. He brought a friend who ran a tourist agency in town. After introductions I explained about visiting Nagaland without a permit. As Prem had business to attend to I thanked him for his help and he left, saying 'B.P. will look after you.' So much for being independent! Apparently, as far as the male species is concerned, a woman on her own in India needs looking after. I conceded that I did need help to enter Nagaland. B.P. took me to the police station for a permit, where the chief of police demanded to know how I had managed to get this far without one!

I told him I used local transport. He questioned me for half an hour after which, and with no progress, I wandered onto the veranda and left the persuading to B.P. The building overlooked the Brahmaputra. Dhobis scrubbed at the clothes on the banks using the large, flat rocks to spread out the washing. A little ferry steamed slowly along the muddy river. My name was called. I could *not* have a permit – Nagaland was off-limits to foreigners. We left the station and set off for B.P.'s agency in a horse and buggy. I was determined to visit Nagaland.

B.P. phoned agencies and airlines on my behalf, but no one would help me without a permit. The next step of my journey was solved by B.P. He was travelling to Khazaranga Wildlife Park to pick up some Americans on a travel familiarisation tour. He could not leave immediately, but arranged a car and driver to take me. I could have an elephant ride in the jungle while waiting for him, before proceeding together to Jorhat. This was excellent. I returned to the lodge in the buggy, and had a good night's sleep now that my problem was solved. I left the next morning with a lovely Assamese lady passenger who was on her way home after shopping. She wore a colourful, bright sari and dangling, gold ear-rings.

KHAZARANGA

On the way, we passed many small villages until we reached her house. As she got out of the car she beckoned to me to join her. It was built of wood and surrounded by an abundance of colourful flowers. Out at the back there was a grassy area, a duck pond and more flowers and trees. The toilet was a rectangular, concrete structure at the side of the garden. It had no sink but there was a bucket of water and a ladle with which to wash one's hands. We had tea, no milk, with delightful snacks and a conversation in Pidgin English, accompanied by many gestures, after which I set off once more for the Park, arriving at 2 p.m. The first voice I heard was loud and American.

'Where have you appeared from? Here is my card. Are you staying the night? We are having a party. You can use my room. I have two spare beds, have a shower.'

I thanked the gentleman and used his bathroom, which had heavenly hot water. Saying 'no' to the party and the bed, I mentioned that I was not staying.

'Where are you going? There is no place to go from here; this is the end of the line.'

'Nagaland.'

'Where's that?'

'East,'

'Never heard of it.' He replied.

I was sitting outside the hotel having a cup of tea when I looked up and saw Jack and Isobel, my train companions. Amazed to meet again, we swopped tales and laughed. I later set off into the jungle with the American party in cars. I handed the guide my letter of introduction from B.P., but I had missed the elephant ride. And though the park is famous for white rhinoceros, I did not see any. There were a variety of strange, colourful birds, a rogue elephant (which we had to stay very still for, until it thundered away), different types of deer and a tiger. After the tour, we returned to the hotel, which consisted of low buildings offering good-sized rooms with en-suite facilities. B.P. arrived after tea. We went to a large tent where guides and travel agents from all over India had gathered to promote tourism, and where there was an unlikely traveller: a Japanese student. *Unlikely* because, at that time, Japanese did not usually travel alone. Here was another adventurer! He had got lost and been taken under the wing of another agent, as I had been by B.P. We swapped stories and wished each other luck. B.P. introduced me to the other agents and I was given the only chair in the room, with the agents quite content to sit cross-legged on the carpet. A bottle of vodka was produced and taken neat. After an interesting chat and handshakes all round, B.P. and I set off in the dark, his chauffeur once more at the wheel. I felt very privileged at having been part of this hospitable group.

A passing image of trees, foliage, strange cries of animals and a long drive, after which we arrived at the Oriental Hotel in Jorhat in time for dinner.

JORHAT

My room was tiny but clean, with an en-suite and a door that opened on to the veranda. B.P. came in, looking very Eastern in a colourful longi. He had dark eyes, bushy black eyebrows and full lips. Well-built, he was about a foot taller than myself. He obviously expected us to dine in the room, with perhaps a romantic interlude. I, however, opted for the dining room. He then changed into shirt and slacks. The Indian men encountered on my travels were so helpful; they never gave me any problems and were kind, hospitable and thorough gentlemen.

The dining room had a threadbare carpet with bench seating. The tables were decked with pure white cloths, just as in any high-class restaurant. B.P. ordered a variety of delicious dishes, naan, daal and spicy vegetables washed down with masala tea. The night was warm, balmy; tropical palms silhouetted against a darkening sky, stars beginning to appear. It was peaceful. I was exhausted after the car journey and retired for the night, to be woken from a deep sleep at 5 a.m. by a terrific noise. A huge, white bird had landed on the roof, wings flapping so I was up and dressed by 6 a.m. Almost everything starts at the crack of dawn in India and the noise precludes further sleep. B.P. was already up and having breakfast, and we discussed how I was to further my journey. He bargained hard with the hotel manager who agreed to provide a car for my trip to Nagaland. Then, after a fond farewell, he departed for Khazaranga and his American travel agents.

I had expected only a driver but a car and two men arrived. B.P. had agreed my fare so I was not worried about paying extra, and with my luggage stowed in the boot I sat in the back and puzzled over the extra man. Half an hour from Jorhat we broke down. The second man was a mechanic. He repaired the problem in twenty minutes and we drove off, stopping in a village for chai. Wooden huts lined the street, flies hummed around the stalls, cattle and dogs wandered around, thin and bony. Curious locals appeared. I needed to use a toilet but could see nothing resembling a hotel amongst the shaky jumble of huts. I wandered up and down, desperately looking for somewhere to conduct my ablutions. Eventually, I consulted the driver who spoke to a stall owner, who spoke to a boy who led me along the road to a house where a missionary lived. Stupidly, I felt embarrassed about marching up to his door demanding to use his loo and so we returned to the stall. When this information was passed to the owner, he accompanied me up the street to a hut behind which was a very muddy patch of ground, surrounded by a high wooden fence. He pointed to a corner, smiled and left. I looked around, decided no one could see me and squatted with relief. As I did so a squeak made me look up to see a face watching me from the door. It withdrew as I rose and hitched up my jeans. When I exited, there were grins from interested spectators and one grin was wider than the rest.

NAGALAND

We continued our journey. The car broke down five miles later. I glared with frustration when I was told that it was necessary for the mechanic to return to the village and since there was little transport on the roads, he had to wait for a passing lorry to hitch a lift. We had stopped beside some tiny cottages and several curious youths on bicycles surrounded the car. I was surprised to see bicycles in this remote area, although, on reflection, it was a good mode of transport considering the lack of buses. Around us were fields, hills and jungle. Chickens and ducks scraped for food in the gardens of the thatched cottages; women carrying young children emerged but were too shy to come near.

One hour later the mechanic returned, repaired the car and we carried on. The road was wide and ran alongside the jungle. Men on elephants directed operations to workers digging and repairing the road. The grey hides of these imposing animals, kept under control by mahouts, were dusty and wrinkled. With raised trunks they lifted trees and dropped them like toys, clearing the road for traffic. I was beginning to wonder if we would ever reach Nagaland or spend the night in the nearby jungle. Finally, however, we rounded a bend to be greeted by a check post. In hindsight I should have expected this. In the falling dusk a policeman left his hut on the hill and peered into the car. The driver presented his papers and I was asked for my passport and name.

The official examined these, then waved us on with a 'Memsahib.'

'Well,' I thought, 'here I am in Nagaland without a hassle! Why was everyone, except me, worried about a permit?' The policeman seemed more concerned about the driver's credentials.

We arrived in Dinapur where the driver asked directions to a hotel. This was a tourist lodge situated on a hill, approximately three miles from a village. When we reached it, the driver demanded Rs.200 extra. I gave him a piece of my mind and they left. The lodge was a long, low, two-storey building with high ceilings. I was very hot, dusty, tired, hungry and thirsty – dying for a cup of tea.

A man appeared, said nothing, lifted my suitcase and beckoned. My room was spacious with stone floors, a ceiling fan, wooden bunk beds, mosquito nets and an en-suite with a cold shower. There were no toilet rolls and no towels – no luxury here then. After a welcome shower I went downstairs to the empty dining room. The same person came and took the order from the smudged menu. There were no other guests and my footsteps sounded hollow in the empty rooms. Tea and toast arrived twenty minutes later. In many remote areas where English is not spoken, gestures and miming were understood. However, there is usually a rudimentary knowledge of the language. By this time, I had picked up some Hindi, but was not always understood, as there were many varying dialects.

I decided to see something of the area. By now it was pitch black, with only one light in the grounds that shone from a little hut at the lodge entrance. Walking to the road I

wondered how I was going to get into town. The only transport I had seen was a scooter trailing a rickshaw. After some
time, car lights approached and I stood in the middle of the
road to flag it down. It was a Jeep, and the driver, who spoke
English, kindly gave me a lift to the market. I wandered
between the shops and stalls lit by oil lamps. I was extremely
hungry and bought delicious vegetable samosas, keeping some
for the next day. On the return journey I hailed a scooter and,
clinging precariously to the pillion, managed not to fall off.

I climbed into bed, let down the mosquito net, read for a
while, turned off the light and attempted to sleep. Mosquitoes
hummed and sang, exotic floral scents wafted in from the
garden and finally dawn crept through the curtain-less window.
Early morning mist curled around the bushes. I showered and
dressed and breakfast was brought to my room; naan and two
hard-boiled eggs. Afterwards, I packed my rucksack and
walked into town.

There were cottages with thatched roofs. Built of clay
embedded in wire mesh, they blended into the countryside.
Children walking to school wrapped in colourful Naga shawls
were otherwise dressed in Western clothing. The town was
further than I expected so, once more, I waved down a scooter,
which took me to the bus station. There, I bought a ticket to
Kohima near the Burmese border, where I might find the ruins
of our old house that, my sister had said, was bombed by the
Japanese during the war. The bus shook as it rattled its way up
the hill from Dinapur. Sacks of goods were strewn in the pas-
sageway; bags of rice rolled around the floor. Hard, wooden
seats made for an uncomfortable journey. I tried to converse
with the lady beside me, admiring her baby, but she just smiled
and shook her head.

A couple of miles out of town we encountered a check post, and, to my dismay, a policeman came on board asking for permits. Here we go again. Evidently, even the local people required these to move round as it was, (I found out later), a politically sensitive area. I quickly covered my hair with a headscarf and gazed out the window, suddenly fascinated by the view. I ignored a tap on the shoulder and the command, 'Come with me', but, with a heavy hand on my person I complied, shouting for the driver to wait for me.

I followed the officer to the roadside hut that was the police post, handed over my passport and confessed to not having a permit. He wanted to know how I had managed thus far without one. Meanwhile, the driver was honking his horn, the passengers were shouting at him to leave and I was shouting at him to wait. Much to my annoyance, the policemen waved him on: the barrier lifted and the bus, my only means of transport, disappeared. The policeman, whose name was Nagen, rang the Dinapur station and was ordered to bring me in.

There were no cars in the vicinity and indeed few in the country, so Nagen stood in the road and commandeered a passing lorry. We joined the driver in his cabin with me squeezed in the middle. Was I a prisoner? When we reached the police station the commissioner was about to get into his car. At that time Indira Gandhi was standing for re-election as prime minister. In several towns in the north there were riots and the commissioner, who was in a hurry to tackle them, had no time for me. He questioned me there and then in the courtyard. I told him I had no guns, no bombs and was merely trying to re-trace my father's footsteps. 'Lock her up', he said, he would deal with me later. The car sped away and with Nagen firmly gripping my arm and passport, I was marched into the police station. I was a prisoner.

In the office the superintendent was seated behind an imposing desk. I was sure this was a relic from the days of the Raj. The interrogation began. I was economical with the truth, not mentioning the names of those who had helped me. The superintendent took copious notes and by the time I had finished my story, he was regarding me with disbelief. He decided I needed guarding and assigned a policeman, complete with rifle, to stand behind me. While he was busy with his notes I wandered to the open back door followed by my guard, to where there was a broken-down Jeep without wheels and sunk in the dried mud – *Naga Flying Squad* painted in white on the bonnet. I could not suppress a giggle and wished I had my camera. Nagen called me back and asked me to sit down to answer more questions.

I was now hungry and thirsty and asked for tea, prior to being locked up. A pot with snacks soon arrived. I took my time drinking, savouring the snacks and desperately thinking. The thought of being a prisoner in a remote country, and my family's distress at the potential consequences, was beginning to take root. To buy more time I said I needed the toilet. This caused consternation – there was no ladies' toilet. I was led to the men's accompanied by my guard Zapu. Back in the office, sipping my tea, it was beginning to filter through that I should be docile – certainly not argumentative. There was a book of laws on a shelf –another relic of the Raj, perhaps –and picking it up I leafed through it. *Abduction*, just what I needed. I asked permission to speak.

I managed to convince the superintendent that the police had abducted me – taken me from the bus against my will. I was starving, dirty and tired and, if I were locked up, it would create an international incident for which he would be responsible. I then had a stroke of genius. I mentioned Rajni, whose surname was Patel – a name synonymous with many ministers of government at that time. I mentioned that I knew him well and he was working for Gandhi throughout the north. After more gentle persuasion I was released into Nagen's custody, to be deported forthwith. Zapu was also assigned to see me onto the first train for Calcutta.

Fortunately, the train was not due for some time. I was hungry and wanted to shop. We stopped at a street stall for spicy dishes – my treat – and thence to the market. I sat on the step of a wooden stall while the owner displayed his wares. I pointed to two colourful shawls, one wool, one silk, and Nagen bargained a 20 per cent discount. The owner wrapped them in brown paper and we left. Feeling embarrassed at having two police escorts with rifles, I asked if one could leave. After a discussion Zapu did so. Nagen hailed two scooters and escorted me to the lodge to pack.

Nagen was tall, broad shouldered and handsome. His cinnamon eyes crinkled when he smiled which he did often, as we had established a good rapport. He was an unusual height. Most Nagas are physically small and favour a ruddy complexion, more Tibetan than Indian, I thought. He told me he was Indian and had been assigned duty in Nagaland. This was now considered part of the parent state of Assam and the created state of Meghalaya on the borders of Assam to the west and Burma to the east. People were not encouraged to move around due to political instability. He would not divulge more but I knew the Nagas had been fighting for independence since 1950. During the Second World War when the Japanese attempted to enter India via Burma, they were defeated by British and Indian armies. The last known headhunting had been in 1960.

At the lodge I was unable to convince Nagen to remain downstairs while I showered and packed. His orders were not to let me out of his sight. What did the officials think I was going to do, climb out a window and escape? The windows were too small. I had already tried to explore and been caught and abducted. I left the bathroom door open as instructed and Nagen turned his back and packed my case – a gentleman. I settled my bill and, once again clinging to a scooter, we arrived at the railway station. Nagen carried my case and I shouldered my rucksack. Two Naga ladies who were walking along the platform stopped and, through my escort, invited me to tea. He refused on my behalf but when I asked him to explain the reason, the ladies scolded him so loudly he was embarrassed. I watched, interested and with no sympathy whatsoever, as a flush crept over his dark complexion. When the train arrived he grabbed my case, found me a seat amongst the hordes of travellers and waved goodbye – no doubt glad to be rid of me.

When the train slowed down at stations children as young as seven ran alongside, shouting the wares that they carried in flat, wicker baskets. I bought samosas to appease my hunger on the long, slow journey and pondered the question: had Shillong been part of Nagaland? If not, then perhaps mother and baby had been transported there after the birth. I drifted off to sleep imagining a bullock cart trundling along a beaten track.

On arrival in Calcutta I waited until the crowds in the train –the noise and shouting, families greeting one another and coolies touting for custom– had dissipated before collecting my luggage. A coolie noticed me. He hoisted my case on to his head and set off at a pace for the taxi rank. I booked into the luxurious Oberoi Hotel for rest and recuperation. A bath with hot water, shampoo, toilet rolls, tissues, real soap, a firm, comfortable mattress and plump soft pillows – bliss.

The End

BHUTAN

I was sitting in a luxury hotel in Calcutta, waiting for breakfast and recovering from the ignominy of having been deported from Nagaland. Leafing through a magazine I looked at photographs of Bhutan. I had never been there but had a Bhutanese friend so the name was not unknown to me. The country had always seemed quite remote but it was not so far from Calcutta and this might be my only chance to visit.

I settled my extortionate bill – thank goodness I had stayed only one night – packed my case, shouldered my rucksack and took a taxi to the airport. I bought a ticket to Bogdugra, the small airport in the north. Once again, I was asked for my permit and was relieved when my passport was accepted instead. I would probably require a permit for Bhutan but, without one, I would take my chances.

Bhutan is a name used by foreigners, the correct name is Druk Yul: Land of the Thunder Dragon. It is a Buddhist country and has many temples, dzongs and monasteries. It sits at the eastern end of the Himalayan mountains, where the dry plains of India meet dense forests. Bhutan is small, and remained isolated for centuries: recently as 1961 entry was by horseback or on foot. After the coronation of His Majesty, Jigme Singye Wangchuk, in 1974, tourism began. The population was approximately 600,000. Indian currency was accepted and at that time Rs.37 equalled less than £1. I intended to enter the country at the border town of Phuntsholing and then travel to Thimpu, the capital and centre of government.

I flew to Bogdugra, sharing a taxi to Siliguri with four other Europeans who were travelling on to Darjeeling. Taxis in India were usually shared as distances were long and therefore expensive. The driver dropped me at a small hotel in this bustling, crowded, noisy town. Stallholders hawked their wares; whole families, perched precariously on the family bicycle, wended a dangerous path in and out of traffic. Bicycle rickshaws and tuk-tuks vied for passengers and sari-clad ladies bargained in the market place. I hired a rickshaw with instructions to be taken to a small hotel. There, I explained that I would like to hire a car to Bhutan for the following morning. The manager said it was a tall order and would probably be expensive but he would do his utmost. I knew that the right amount of money could solve most problems and was prepared to pay a commission. Besides, the manager would extract a further commission from the driver.

The next morning, after a great deal of haggling I hired a car for Rs.700. Leaving my case at the hotel; I hefted my rucksack, climbed into the back seat and set off with Suri the driver. There were several check posts along the way, which, fortunately, were unmanned. With some urging on my part Suri, who tended to stop at them, drove straight through.

Finally, after four hours, we arrived at the border and another unmanned check post. We drove straight on into Phuntsholing. We had been very lucky to enter without being stopped. I breathed a sigh of relief.

Suri was not happy at leaving me on my own but I thanked him, assured him I was quite safe, paid my fare, and watched him drive away. I booked into the Hotel Nangay and went straight to bed, tired from the long, dusty journey. The next morning, after a breakfast of toast, boiled egg and tea, I received directions to the bus station where I bought a ticket for Thimpu. By 7 a.m. the bus was full and we left.

We had not travelled far when we stopped at a check post – how tiresome these were and seemed to be everywhere in the north. A customs' officer came on board to examine permits. I handed over my passport only to be told to leave the bus. I accompanied the officer to the immigration post where, surprisingly, everyone spoke very good English. I was informed that without a permit I was not allowed to go further and should return to the border and leave. I sat down in the corner of the veranda to await a bus. Bhutanese officers were playing a game on a small, wooden table with what looked like snooker cues, shunting small tiles around. It resembled a type of pool.

The men wore the national dress, gho, which put one in mind of a knee-length dressing gown tied at the waist. Knee-high socks and sturdy boots completed the uniform. Women wore a kira, which is ankle length of acrylic or Kashmir wool. After two hours an officer asked me why I was there. He informed me that there was no more local transport. He then pointed to an official who was just leaving in a chauffeur-driven car and said that I should ask for a lift to the Ministry of Foreign Affairs where I could apply for a permit. This sounded hopeful.

On arrival and after a lengthy interview the minister asked me if I knew anyone in Bhutan. This was obviously a prerequisite for entry. Tongue in cheek I mentioned my friend, who was entirely unknown to the minister but after some persuasion I was granted my permit for US$20, and walked back to the hotel ,ecstatic. Early next morning I was on the bus once more. This time it was an express bus, leaving at 7 a.m. and arriving in Thimpu at 1.45 p.m.

The journey was a breath-taking drive round hairpin bends, long winding roads leading into the Inner Himalayas where passes reach 12,000 feet, with often a sheer drop on one side and mountain on the other. The driver stopped at a viewpoint overlooking the meeting of the Paro and Thimpu rivers and the Paro valley, where houses were clustered along the riverside. As we continued, trees and scrub covered the rocky hills, becoming sparser as we approached Thimpu. On arrival, I inspected a few hotels before choosing the Hotel Tandin, which was fairly new and where I was given a room for a discounted price of Rs.180. There was no water for a shower, but there was the luxury of a fan heater in this cold country.

At reception, I inquired about trekking. I wanted to see as much of the country as possible in the week I had been allowed. Venturing into the interior with a group would cost US$80 a day – beyond my budget. The next day, in a tracksuit and fleece, I bought mineral water, cheese and bread, shouldered my rucksack and set off into the surrounding hills.

The hill I chose was riven with deep grooves which, from below, I had mistaken for tracks. They were caused by logs that the local teenagers, when gathering kindle, tied together at one end and dragged down the hill. I was told there was an abundance of wildlife, although I did not have the pleasure of spotting any. Hunting was forbidden. The pine trees had very soft long needles; some were so pale as to be almost white, with many cones. Many were slashed and oozing a sticky substance. Walking was easy. The soil was dry and appeared to have some iron pyrite (otherwise known as fool's gold) scattered around. I returned along the river track and noticed crops of maize, wheat, rice and chillies. Traffic was mostly official cars, motorbikes and Land Rovers – the latter probably belonging to the aid agencies whose offices I saw: V.S.O. UNICEF, Netherlands, the U.N. The houses were varied, some of brick with cement overlay and attractive, wooden, arched windows, some clay with tin roofs weighted down with stones. The older ones were used for storing hay. I passed a *dzong*, a huge stone building with wooden decoration along the roof, perhaps a headquarters of sorts and which I was not allowed to enter. An official, who was coming out, asked me why I was in Bhutan. When I explained that I was a tourist travelling on my own, he decided I was secretly researching hotels for tourism in the West. So be it, I thought, one obviously needs a role to be here and that will be mine.

I met a party of school children on their way to a picnic who produced a camera. They were extremely polite, asking questions about the outside world and speaking good English, which was taught in the schools. There was a *chorten* which was locked, but the locals walked around it several times chanting 'OM' and fingering beads. Prayer flags on long poles fluttered in the wind, carrying mantras on the breeze. There seemed to be no objection to foreigners: many Indian businessmen and consultants were here. The wealthier locals had houses on the hillsides and I was told an amusing story – that the wealthy grew potatoes and smuggled out musk with the crop. I watched men practise archery, a favourite sport. By the river, women were hunched over a very large stone, holding a thick metal band into which they inserted a smaller stone. Using this rudimentary tool, they hammered the bigger one to gravel – a gruelling task. Workmen's tools were primitive and huge pieces of timber were planed manually. I decided it was time to return to my hotel for a shower and dinner as my nose was turning an unbecoming purple from an overdose of sun.

I reached the hotel dirty, hungry and cold but as there was no water from the shower a bucket of hot water was brought to my room. The loo worked once in the morning and once at night. Below the sink, a plastic hose was connected to run the water into a drain, but it did not. There was not more than a trickle to wash clothes, so it was fortunate that I had brought paper disposable pants! Dinner was delicious, plain boiled rice, vegetables and a spicy meat dish and noodles. Fish was also on the menu. Siliguri is a tea-growing area and pots of nice tea were served. There was a technical college in Thimpu for apprentice tradesmen, although some young people go to India for tertiary education.

Bhutan was progressing and yet the government did not wish tourists to flood the country, as had occurred in Nepal, as this would change the way of life which, in 1978, was peaceful. When I spoke to the director of Etho Metho tours and explained I was on my own, she was surprised. Visitors are invited or apply in groups for trekking; single travellers are not encouraged. The hotel staff were very good – not charging for endless cups of tea. Dinner was Rs.37 and mineral water Rs.15. Many shops operated as bars with liquor freely available, as were English cigarettes. According to letters in the local paper, garbage and toilets were a problem. I was told there was a swimming pool but could not find it. Where did the water come from? I could have done with some. Keen to buy a gold charm for my daughter, I found a jeweller. He was sitting cross-legged on a mat in front of his hut a dying log fire with glowing embers beside him, ready for business. The tools of his trade were hanging on a plank of wood fixed to a wall, his weights and measures displayed on the mat with a small iron block resembling an anvil. He told me that he had no gold in stock, but if I left an order he could fulfil it.

I had enjoyed my stay –the hotel, the food, the friendly people –but my visa had expired. I left the following morning at 7:30 for Phuntsoling. With no time to stay in the Nangay another night I telephoned the hotel to ask them to buy a ticket for the express bus to Siliguri.

The bus was full, and it was an uncomfortable journey as I was leaning on someone's suitcase and jammed in between the driver and three other passengers. We arrived at 1.15 p.m. I dashed to the hotel to collect my case and ticket, as the bus was due to leave at 3:30. I was informed that, as there was a strike on the Indian side, the border was closed and the hotel had been unable to buy a ticket for me. I was overstaying my visa but, if I was not going to be deported, I did not mind. I felt I needed some luxury and booked into the more upmarket Hotel Druk for Rs.250 – a 15 per-cent discount. I showered the dust off with hot water, washed my hair and a pair of socks and enjoyed a dinner of *keera desh*, plain rice and naan.

The road opened the next day. I took the bus to Siliguri and a taxi to Bogdugra for a flight to Delhi. On arrival, I expected to fly Air India to Hong Kong without difficulty. This was not about to happen. The next flight was in two days. I was running short of money, but fortunately my flights had been pre-booked and pre-paid. What to do in the middle of the night and with no transport into town? The airport manager provided a rest room underneath the airport car park. I was very tired but sleep was impossible because the security men on guard duty nattered all night then knocked on doors to find out when passengers were leaving. I was not the only one to have missed a flight. At dawn I was told to leave and check into a hotel as these rooms were reserved for late-night arrivals only.

I picked up my case and scruffy backpack and made my way, by local bus, into Delhi booking into a grotty hotel for a whopping Rs.440. I was very hungry and had *paratha* and *sag paneer* for lunch. After a shower I tried to catch up on sleep but the noise outside prevented this and I went for a walk instead.

The next morning, I caught a bus to the airport and flew home to Hong Kong.

The End

FINDING GRANDMOTHER

My grandmother had died in India and I wanted to visit her grave. My dilemma was that although I knew from relatives that she languished in a grave somewhere in Calcutta, I had no idea where she was buried. My parents had never spoken of her except to say that she had died of smallpox. With no more information other than my maiden name, I decided to fly via Bombay, to see as much of India as possible.

I arrived on an August night. Feeling shattered after the long flight I staggered off the plane to go through immigration, collected my suitcase and proceeded to customs where I was questioned regarding Indian currency. Through my ignorance I carried a substantial number of Indian rupees. The officer demanded that I hand them over, as it was illegal to enter the country with them. An argument developed. After half an hour of this, the official told me to stay put as he wished to consult his superior, and he disappeared through a door. As he did so, I picked up my suitcase and exited the building into the bustling street of taxi drivers and coolies.

I beckoned a driver who took possession of my case, pushing aside porters and coolies as he stowed it in the boot. I settled inside the car, which shook and rattled its way into the city that was quiet at this time of night. Half-dozing I was jerked awake by the taxi stopping. Three times the driver stopped and asked directions, by which time I was becoming suspicious. I was to stay at a hotel in Bandar Abbas Road, but he drove into unlit streets where he cut the engine and drifted into a cul-de-sac. He applied the brakes and hissed 'baksheesh' (money). I ignored him, so he leaned over and repeated it in a loud voice. Just then there were noises from outside and when I looked out of the window I saw, to my amazement, bundles of rags moving. The place was littered with street sleepers and he had almost run over one, missing his head by a whisker. I opened the taxi door and shouted at the driver so that the sleepers, who were now awake and annoyed, could hear me. They rose up in a bedraggled mob and converged on the taxi. Frightened, he switched on the engine, backed out and turned into Bandar Abbas Road. I tumbled out and spoke to the guard at the hotel who collected my case and severely reprimanded the driver. I did not pay.

After this experience I was disenchanted with Bombay and, after a day wandering around the city, flew to Calcutta.

Every year the monsoon winds of July and August bring the rains on which India's teeming population depend. I was foolhardy enough to land in Calcutta in the middle of them, in intense heat and humidity. I caught the local bus from the airport into town. It trundled along flooded streets as rain battered against the windows until it finally slowed down and stopped. Darkness descended. Seeing no alternative, I climbed down into the swirling waters, suitcase in hand, and sloshed through to the pavement where a rickshaw coolie squatted, waiting for a customer. I gave the hotel address and he set off, barefoot, a bandana wound round his forehead and wearing only a loin-cloth.

Spray from the large wheels slapped at my face as I cowered under the hood. Ladies in brilliant saris waded along the pavement, hands holding up their garments in a forlorn attempt to keep them dry. Stallholders sat hunched on high stools amidst colourful wares, waving cheerily as we rolled by. Eventually the waters receded as we approached the hotel and the coolie's face split into a grin as I added a large tip.

'Ah cha, memsahib', he said, his head shaking vigorously as he sped off into the night.

I was confronted by a set of large, black gates, which I shook vigorously, at the same time shouting, as there was no bell. The *chowkidar*, rubbing sleep from his eyes finally arrived and demanded to know my identity before opening the gates. Midnight had come and gone, and I was soaked, tired and hungry. After booking in and drinking a welcome cup of tea with toast, I retired for the night.

This establishment, set in the centre of an overpopulated city, beside old, tall buildings, markets, street sleepers and beggars, is an anachronism - a throwback to the days of the Raj. It was a very large bungalow set in a garden, and was originally owned by two sisters who started it as a hotel. The rooms had wooden floors and wooden ceiling fans which lazily swept through the air, re-arranging the dust motes. The wooden stairs had accommodated multitudinous footsteps. The dining room had previously been the withdrawing room, but now waiters wearing black pants, white jackets and gloves glided silently among the tables. There was a sense of quiet and peace.

The next day dawned sunny, hot and humid. I hailed a taxi to the old cemetery and my grandmother's grave, unaware that there were several old cemeteries in Calcutta. Entering through a gate and stone arch, I saw a padlocked door and a notice – 'Closed until 3 p.m. Caretaker'. Three men lay on charpoys but did not move when I spoke. Not much help there then. The cemetery was completely overgrown, the grass high, the surrounding walls covered in ivy. Flat grave stones, marble slabs, tombs with domed roofs built in a semi-circle erected to the dead of whole families, wife, husband, children, many who had died of malaria, typhoid, or smallpox like my grand-mother. With no idea where she lay I started up one path and down another, trying not to miss any. Dozens of crows perched, cawed and hopped from tomb to tomb as if pulling me onwards. Goats stood on slabs and chewed the foliage. By now I was ankle-deep in water and mud. Fortunately, I had foreseen this and was wearing plastic sandals with my slacks rolled up. There were carvings: infants of three months, six-year olds and young newlyweds. I tried to make out times and dates but many of the graves were disintegrating and others broken; some had no visible writing at all. I trod down the grass and started at one end of the wall tearing at the ivy, trying not to think of snakes. I slapped at mosquitoes relishing fresh blood, and shook a sleeping coolie awake so I could read the slab he was reclining on. Eventually I sank down on a stone verge, exhausted: four hours searching without success. I washed my feet and sandals in a pool of water, rolled down my slacks and left, disappointed.

Further down the road, to my surprise, I discovered another cemetery with a caretaker in residence, who asked if he could help. I told him I was ancestor-hunting. When I said I could supply only my maiden name and nationality he clicked his tongue at my inefficiency. He produced a register, but could not find the name Dempster. Seeing my misery, he suggested that, since my grandparents were Scottish, I should visit St. Andrew's Church in Dalhousie Square –where the minister would direct me to the Scottish cemetery. I mentioned that I had just left there, at which he shook his head and informed me that that was the English cemetery. Well, I thought, if ever I catch that taxi driver I'll strangle him. I thanked the caretaker and with a spark of hope, took the two-hour tram ride to the church. It was closed. A notice proclaimed it was open from 9.30 a.m. to 12.30 p.m. It was 5.30 p.m. I walked all the way round, but could not find an entrance. Exhausted and hungry I sat in a tiny restaurant across the road at the back of the church where *chapattis*, *daal* and tea soon restored my energy and humour.

I returned to the church next morning. Classical music resounded, bouncing off the walls. There were two men. The one sitting behind a large desk introduced himself as the Reverend Noel Sen and his helper, Robin. Both were extremely helpful when I explained the situation. I had no idea when my grandmother had died so we started with records from 1915 to 1934. To find information the Reverend – 'call me Noel!'– had to fetch ladders to reach dusty ledgers resting on a high shelf. He brought down a tome. As I looked through the register Noel served Earl Grey tea while Mozart, Mendelssohn, Verdi and Rossini played. I ran my finger down the dates and names, flicking over pages in anticipation. As I neared the end my heart dropped to my shoes. Nothing. The next tome – 1934 -36 – nothing. Nothing between 1913 and 1916. We decided to start from the beginning of the century and down came ledger number four. As we discussed what to do next if we did not find it, I suddenly grabbed Noel's hand. There it was: 1909 – Mary Dempster, died of smallpox aged 38. I wanted to take a photograph so Robin carried the book out into the sunlight.

Noel was as pleased as I was, and offered to send Robin with me to the Scottish cemetery which was distanced from the other cemeteries I had visited. We caught a taxi.

The cemetery name was written on the outside on yellow coloured walls covered in graffiti. As we entered, the caretaker, who lived in a small building by the gate, came out to help: without a plot number it was going to be a difficult task. I gazed around to find that it was even more overgrown than the English cemetery. Goats chewing the long grass were perched on the graves. Crows cawed, mosquitoes bit and snakes slithered away as we started our search. The caretaker and a coolie carrying a scythe went in one direction and we went in another. Then, as I was pulling at grass and ivy, tearing up roots, wading through puddles and slipping on gravestones hidden in the undergrowth, a shout from the caretaker told us he had found the grave. Robin and I rushed over and there it was. The coolie scythed away the remainder of the grass to leave it clear.

IN MEMORY OF ROBERT STEVENSON
WHO DIED IN AYR, SCOTLAND IN 1908
AND OF MARY DEMPSTER
WHO DIED IN 1909
Buried by her husband Robert Dempster

I had difficulty in seeing anything at that moment as the tears rolled down my cheeks. I thanked everyone profusely for their efforts and stood alone by the rectangular marble slab, split down the middle with age. Roots were poking through. I read the inscription and realised I had found two relatives, Robert Stevenson, who was my great-grandfather. At the top of the slab was a heavy, pyramid-shaped stone with four marble torches facing downwards, one at each corner. There was a hole at the top where something else had sat. The caretaker explained that grave robbers would have stolen it, as it was good Italian marble. I sat and contemplated. If India had been the jewel in the crown of the British Empire many had paid dearly for it – Indian and British alike. When I enquired about the state of the cemetery the caretaker explained that it was impossible to keep the grass short throughout the year, as it grew so quickly; however, after the monsoon season it was cut and every stone cleared of foliage. He told me that a lady was carrying out research on the cemetery and was writing a book. There were 1,800 graves and she had noted all the names.

Robin and I returned to St Andrew's to pick up the reverend who had invited me to the Swimming Pool Club. On arrival we joined a table of six men and enjoyed a celebratory whisky. During lunch Noel nudged me good humouredly and said, 'We Indians were not allowed here in the days of the Raj.' 'Touché,' I said, and we clinked glasses. After a delicious lunch I returned to the cemetery with a dozen peach roses bought from a street stall. I scattered them over the grave, said my farewell, and handed baksheesh to the caretaker to thank him for his efforts. With the help of all these wonderful people my quest was complete. It had taken two days, but had seemed much longer.

The End

NEPAL

My friend Smita, who worked in Bihar in north-west India and who I had not seen for a very long time, wrote, suggesting we meet in Kathmandu. I had never visited Nepal, so this appealed to me.

In 1978, I flew Thai airways to Bangkok and on to Kathmandu with Royal Nepal Airlines.

After landing I caught a bus into town. A night at the Crystal Hotel was expensive, but would enable me to have a shower and tumble into bed after a very long and tiring day. Also, I was using this address for contact with my friend. There was no mail waiting for me so I went to bed. During the night there was a noise in the vicinity of the door. I crept silently across the room and opened it a crack to see a man lying across the threshold, evidently guarding me from intruders, but fast asleep. By morning my watchman had disappeared. After breakfast I looked for and found a cheaper hotel called The Nook. I retraced my steps, packed my bag and checked out of the Crystal. There was still no mail. Meanwhile I hired a bicycle for Rs.5 and set out to explore Kathmandu.

I cycled down narrow back streets with shops on both sides, noisy, happy smiling people, houses crowding in on one another, cars honking, bicycle bells ringing, buses swinging dangerously around corners, pony traps click-clacking, and delicious, mouth-watering curry aromas wafting from the restaurants. I rode out of town and across the Basmati River to a Hindu temple. Entry was barred to non-Hindus so I returned to town and visited the Monkey Temple, leaving my bike at the bottom of some steps. As I climbed I stepped into a curio shop and met Manu, the owner. He volunteered to close his shop and show me around. First stop, the Tibetan lamas who lived in the temple and who were sitting on cushions playing musical instruments, one of which was an enormous, long, tube-like horn stretching yards in front of the lama who was holding it. When we reached the temple roof, Manu gave me a few lessons on meditation, after which we parted. Climbing back down the steps, someone called to me and I saw some lads resting on the grass. One asked me if I smoked and rather naïvely I said yes. He then handed me a small transparent packet containing hash. I looked at these young men – a mixture of nationalities – their eyes were half closed and they were barely capable of raising their heads. I threw the packet on the ground in disgust and walked away amid catcalls. Retrieving my bike, I cycled to Durbar Square. The great stone buildings were surrounded by Westerners in hippy gear, sitting, drinking and smoking. Hash was obviously easily available and cheap.

Next morning I went to see Isobel who worked at the Tiger Tops office whom I had met on a previous trip to India. She insisted I visit Tiger Tops, an animal and nature reserve in the jungle. Flying would be faster than by road. I agreed and having paid for my ticket returned to the hotel, packed a small overnight bag and set out for the airport. I watched a tiny aeroplane land and hoped, in vain, that it was not mine. As I walked across the tarmac a man rushed out of the office with a small sack containing mail, which he handed to me to deliver to Tiger Tops. Once on board I counted the seats: there were ten and, if that was not enough, fold-up seats were located at the end of each row. The pilot climbed in, the engine roared and we soared into the air. Looking down I could see crops growing on the hillsides. Before we had flown very far the pilot announced that we were turning back because students were rioting on the airstrip at Tiger Tops. So it was goodbye yet again to my elephant ride and Tiger Tops experience. Returning the mail sack to the airport attendant he explained this had never happened before – what bad luck.

The following day I enquired at the Crystal Hotel for mail and as none had arrived, decided not to wait for my friend. The Himalayas looked so inviting and majestic I wanted to trek. But first, I had a party to attend, courtesy of Isobel, who picked me up and drove me to her friend's house. Her friend was a beautiful, petite blonde girl from Iceland whose husband was one of the first to set up trekking in the area. I did not meet him but met a lovely family: a white Russian, along with his wife, son and daughter-in-law. He had once owned the Yak and Yeti I was informed. His son and wife had recently returned from two years at a temple in India, and the son was now entitled to wear a saffron robe. His wife had started a Montessori school for Western children in Kathmandu. It was very interesting. I was fascinated to meet such diverse people although we did have an argument during a discussion about love. The general consensus of opinion was that when one learned to love oneself, only then could one love others. I thought this was rather selfish but was informed that 'I hadn't got it'. I had to agree. When the time came to leave and everyone kissed each other, I took two steps back.

As we drove back I told Isobel of my plan to trek. She recommended a very reasonable agency that I went to the following day. The owner, who was an ex-Ghurkha soldier from Hong Kong, asked for my passport, which I reluctantly handed over. As he began to question me, I realised that he wanted to know my age and whether I was fit. I replied that I played a lot of sport especially hockey and walked a great deal. When he saw that I was becoming angry at being asked personal questions, he explained that he was responsible for trekkers and if I had an accident in the mountains and required the services of a helicopter I would need to be able to pay for it. We reached an agreement after a heated discussion in which I told him that I had not come to Nepal to finish up in a hospital. (I later learned that he needed to know how many people to send with me as they may have been required to carry me back to civilisation). For US$30 a day I would have a bearer, a cook and a guide. Impatient, I wanted to start the next day but we eventually settled on the day after. On my way back to the hotel I discovered a restaurant called K.C.'s where delicious food was on offer: spaghetti, cheese, pies and cakes. Marvellous.

I spent the next day shopping for suitable gear and, carrying only a rucksack, presented myself at the office where I was introduced to my team. There was Ang Kami, my Sherpa and guide – a wiry five-ft. 6 in. with a ready smile and 35-years old, at a guess. The cook (Cookie) was an older, well-built man with a toothy grin and weather-beaten skin; the bearer was slight and young. I wondered if he would manage to carry his share of the food and utensils that were to be conveyed in two elongated cone-shaped rattan baskets. One of these would be carried on his back, supported by a band around his head.

We set off by bus to the Pokhara Valley and the Annapurna Range. Loaded on to the roof were our two large baskets containing food, cooking equipment, tents and sleeping bags. Cookie carried a lamp. When we arrived at Pokhara, Ang Kami handed me a *Lemu*, a lemon drink – perhaps the equivalent of Coca-Cola in the mountains? I thought it was ghastly and could not finish it. We set forth walking in a line – Ang Kami first, me next, then the cook and bearer each carrying a basket. We advanced a short way along the path and into a field where two tents were pitched. One was for my team and the other for me. I considered this an anti-climax. I wanted to be up in the mountains, not sitting three paces from a busy path. When I mentioned this to Ang Kami he just smiled, told me to be patient and to get some sleep. The night was beautiful, with a clear navy-blue sky and thousands of stars glittering above the distant snow-topped mountains with no electric lighting to mar the view. Needless to say I did not sleep well, being unused to tents and hard ground. I dozed off towards dawn and was wakened by a call from outside as the guide placed a bowl of hot water on the ground for my ablutions. Thrusting my hand out, I took the bowl and crouched uncomfortably inside to wash. Soon after, another shout, and my breakfast was brought to the tent.

I gazed at the dishes in amazement. There was porridge – yuk! Although a Scot, I disliked porridge. There was toast, butter and marmalade, eggs, biscuits and a tin mug of tea, complete with milk and sugar. I had expected to rough it but instead was being very well looked after. I drank the tea and nibbled at the toast. Ang Kami eventually collected the tray and returned to say that Cookie was extremely upset I had not eaten much. I explained that I seldom ate breakfast but would happily consume a *chapatti* and tea. Perhaps Cookie was used to catering for strapping males with hearty appetites. I wondered then how much extra weight was being carried unnecessarily in those baskets.

After breakfast, Ang Kami and I set off leaving Cookie and Palu, the bearer, to pack up and follow on. We walked through the Pokhara Valley with the great mountains rearing up on either side. The valley was a flat plain with loose, scattered stones. I heard a jingling of bells and saw a procession of mules and donkeys making their way towards us. The men who sat astride the donkeys wore brown, hide coats and colourful head-gear. We stepped aside to let them pass. They were a merry group, who shouted greetings to the guide. Here and there, stood small huts selling tea and snacks. Two very tall, and very well-built blond men coming down off the hills stopped at one of these huts and placed three rucksacks against the wall. Ang Kami joined their guide at my request to ask why there were three rucksacks. He discovered that three men had gone up into the mountains, but one had been killed while climbing.

We pushed on and I encountered my first hill. By this time, the others were not far behind. I went first. I supposed that Ang Kami did not want to set the pace or I would never have kept up. He was carrying my heavy rucksack and I shouldered a colourful Tibetan bag, purchased locally. This was definitely the way to trek! We eventually reached what I assumed to be the top, but, sitting down with a sigh of relief, I was told that there were a few more hills to climb. Up, up we went between the trees, out onto grassy slopes until finally we came to a flat-topped patch of grass already occupied by two tents. A hut stood some yards away on the opposite side and a pool was nearby. At a nod from my guide, Cookie started a fire and very soon I was drinking a cup of sweet tea. While the evening meal was being prepared, I looked around and noticed an elderly couple sitting outside their tent. I introduced myself to Jean and Lou from America. They were enjoying a three-day trek and had an entourage of seven. After some time, I excused myself for privacy in the bushes but Jean told me to use their 'john.' This rather confused me but they pointed up the hill where, sitting on the top, was a tall, narrow, pyramid-shaped tent. Not wanting to appear ungrateful I climbed the hill with everyone knowing where I was going. Had I disappeared into the bushes no one would have noticed! Inside the pyramid was a hole in the ground dug out by their bearers.

After dinner I heard a scream and ran to the tent where I found Jean in a state of shock! She had returned from the john, bleeding. They called for their guide, who told her to strip and there, on her back, was a leech! The creature was clinging on tenaciously, fat, sleek and black, glistening in the light of the lamp. The guide pulled it off and she felt decidedly sick. Well, a john was one luxury I could do without! It was 9 p.m., and I was about to retire when Ang Kami appeared from a hut with a drink of the local brew made from barley. It was strong and slightly bitter. I entered my tent, secured the flap and crawled into my sleeping bag.

I tried to read by the light of a candle but soon gave up and fell asleep. I awoke abruptly to thunder and lightning crashing through the mountains and a drip, drip, drip on my face. Reaching for the candle I encountered a pool of water and so climbed out of my sleeping bag, untied the flap with difficulty and squelched over to the men's tent. I informed them that I was very wet and that my tent was torn. The guide lit a lamp and went to investigate then he fetched his own sleeping bag and escorted me to the hut, where he awakened the lady of the house. She kindly took me in, cleared a space on the floor beside her family, and made a cup of hot, sweet tea. So I spent my first night under a roof. Everyone was up at the crack of dawn and I had to do without ablutions. Cookie served *chapatti* and another cup of hot, sweet tea – this was turning out to be my survival drink. Jean, Lou, their guide, cook and seven bearers all left with cheery waves. Not one to waste time, Ang Kami had me on the path as soon as I had finished breakfast.

While walking we skirted the pool and to my dismay I saw tiny wee worms disappearing into the three small holes in my trainers. My guide was quickly beside me, pushing me down onto the grass, as he whipped off my shoes. He shook them, and picked off the wee worms, which were in fact leeches preparing to suck my blood! I found it difficult to believe that these tiny, wriggly innocuous-looking things could become the engorged, sleek, black, repulsive creatures on Jean. We started up again – always up –comforted by the thought that what goes up must come down. I managed to push my way onwards and upwards through trees, bushes and exceptionally beautiful scenery. The air was clean and fresh. The Nepalese we passed on the way put their hands together and murmured 'namaste', a lovely greeting roughly translated as 'I bow to the divine spark within you'. We passed many villages connected by steep steps, strung out on the way up the mountain. Children ran up these steps nonchalantly while I laboured to reach the top. Nepal had (at that time) a population of approximately 12 million. Roughly 800,000 lived in Kathmandu and the others in villages spread throughout the country.

When we stopped for lunch Ang Kami spread out my wet sleeping bag on some rocks to dry and Cookie opened a tin of ham, which he served with local vegetables. Thankfully the path was now downhill through bushes and across a river. The sun was hot and fierce and as I burn very easily I slathered lotion on my face. In fact, because of the sun I wore long-sleeved t-shirts with a hat and occasionally a scarf half-covering my face, cowboy fashion! What a sight I must have been. When we had trekked for some time we stopped at a village. My guide studied the sky, pronounced confidently that a storm was brewing and that he would secure a room for me in a lodge. Remembering the previous night I readily agreed. These lodges, high in the Himalayas, were usually run by Gurkha women many of whose husbands were still in the army. They offered the trekker food and a bed very cheaply. My lodge consisted of two floors: downstairs was the kitchen and upstairs a dormitory that both men and women shared. Fortunately there was a small room adjoining which I slept in. I climbed into my sleeping bag, aching in every limb. The rain descended, battering the tin roof as I snuggled down further. The days might be warm but the closer we got to the top the nights were getting ever chillier.

Dawn brought Ang Kami with a bowl of hot water and a cup of hot, sweet tea which I drank sitting on the roof outside the window. The sun rose over the mountains to the dawn chorus. The peace and silence were deep. Going to wash, I found I was covered in blood, Panic stricken I called for Ang Kami who, unzipping my sleeping bag and opening it wide, discovered, nestling in the corners and seams, countless leeches! They must have crawled in while the bag was drying on the rocks. We set out into the early morning sunlight and mist. I was panting and puffing and walking so slowly that Cookie and Palu soon caught up. Lunch was eaten by a river that cascaded down from the mountain, freezing water roaring and swirling by. I perched on a huge boulder with a massive plateful of chips, meat and roast potatoes and, as I sat there, three Australians stopped to chat. It transpired that they had no guide and were lost, and wanted to know if my guide would direct them to the nearest village. While we chatted I held out my laden plate and my lunch rapidly disappeared. Apparently they had not eaten properly for a week. With a handful of chips and potatoes each they headed off. Cookie packed up and we were soon on the move too.

The going became very steep and tough: the path had disintegrated. We were reduced to crawling – grasping at roots to pull us up, the earth slipping away as we did so. I glanced back and saw Cookie slowly slipping downhill, basket on his back and one hand still clutching the kerosene lamp. Fortunately Palu was behind him and managed to arrest his descent. He recovered and advanced, his great boots digging into the rubble. I wondered at the stamina of these Nepalese.

Whenever we sat down to rest there would be a square stone wall, just the right height for the porters to sit down and ease the straps from their foreheads, resting the baskets on the top. Once, as we passed one of these resting places I noticed a figure in white lying down. Greeting the man, he sat up, revealing himself to be an emaciated European with a raging fever. He had no rucksack and told me that he had been trekking with friends when he became ill and could go no further. His friends had taken his bag for him along to the nearest village where he was due to join them when he felt fit enough. He didn't look like he would ever be well enough but I gave him some water and we left. Ang Kami was becoming impatient with my sympathy toward strangers. He scolded me, telling me not to talk to them.

The children we met were lovely. Big brown eyes, ragged clothes, tousled hair, hands reaching out for sweets. No sweets, only pens. With wide smiles and flashing teeth, they would disappear as quickly as they had appeared. As we passed through villages my guide would ask me what I fancied for dinner and would then barter for the ingredients. Cookie would set up camp, get busy with his knives, pots and pans and begin to cook an excellent meal. By this point in the trek my dirty clothes were piling up and Ang Kami mentioned that Palu would happily launder them for me. I didn't mind the idea of his washing my slacks and t-shirts but I was certainly not handing over my underwear! We stopped at a river where I washed my smalls in the freezing water until my hands were blue and my fingers numb. I assumed we were in a remote area, so I strung them on the tent strings to dry. However, as we ate dinner villagers passed by, huge smiles creasing their faces. I did not sleep well. The frequent noise of cows and goats was sufficient to keep me awake. Rising in the middle of the night to relieve myself, I stumbled around in the dark, remembering not to squat too low because of the dreaded leeches and other insects lurking in the undergrowth.

As we climbed I was amazed to see the crops that grew at this height: millet, barley, potatoes, and greens. There was no shortage of food. One of the most moving sights was a husband carrying a basket the Nepali way, a strap round his forehead. He was not carrying food, or firewood, but his wife. She sat erect, emotionless, both hands clutching the sides of the basket. I looked enquiringly at my guide. He told me that since there was no hospital for many miles, this was the method used to take sick villagers for treatment. I wondered how this population survived without facilities such as electricity, telephones, doctors and proper sanitation.

That night we camped near a village. I told my guide I was going to a lodge to seek some English-speaking travellers. He was not happy to let me go on my own and therefore accompanied me. A fire burned in the middle of the room and several nationalities sat around it, drinking tea, and chatting. I found out that many of them were sick and living in the dormitory, for which they paid a pittance. We left them, and I commented to Ang Kami that, so far, the only people we had met were sick or lost. He explained that the locals who owned the lodges re-used tea leaves countless times and if food was not consumed it was kept, without a fridge, until eaten. Also, many travellers climbed without a guide or bearer because, in their opinion, it was spending money unnecessarily. I noticed these trekkers quenching their thirst from pipes that protruded from dykes. Really the only pure water was at the snow line and, along with the poor sanitation, this meant that, unless you were willing to pay Rs.4 for *Lemu* you were drinking contaminated water.(I had now acquired a taste for Lemu) Many travellers died en-route, I was told, and I came across one man who collapsed as he walked.

Palu pitched camp and I went to sleep, only to be washed out again. Ang Kami arranged for me to sleep in the dormitory lodge – no single room this time. I curled into my sleeping bag but woke up during the course of the night– I just had to go to the loo. Trying to sneak outside quietly was impossible as the bed creaked. I stumbled over someone's rucksack, feeling out for the double doors that had to be unbolted and positively thundered on opening. Once outside, a pack of dogs ran around me, followed me up the path to the bushes as I went slipping and sliding on the muddy grass and eventually squatting. I returned to the lodge, still accompanied by my barking hounds. This trip was becoming an obstacle course.

The next morning, I returned to camp for a cup of hot, sweet tea with *chapatti* and a hard-boiled egg. We climbed in the cool of the morning, frequently joined by villagers making their way to other villages. Two little girls scampered up the steep slopes, looking back and shouting 'Grandfather' at two young Germans who were doing their best to keep up but failing miserably. The higher one climbed, the thinner the air became and the more difficult the breathing. We reached a fairly flat wooded area where there were snow monkeys sitting in the trees. White, with black-ringed eyes and long, curly tails, they peered at us from between the branches with wide, curious eyes. When we arrived at the next village Ang Kami met up with some of his Sherpa friends who were guiding other trekking parties – the majority of which consisted of four or more trekkers. Once camp was pitched the guides met in the house of a Gurkha officer serving with the British army whose wife ran a café used only by the guides and bearers. I followed them into the house and sat quietly in a corner, where I was offered *chang*, the local brew. Nobody seemed to mind my presence. A hammock was slung from the roof and the grandfather of the family gently rocked his sleeping grandson.

After this, it was the homeward journey and Cookie's load was now considerably lighter. Our next pitch was at the periphery of a village. Ang Kami and I paid a visit to a lodge where we met a French couple so thin one wondered how they had managed to walk this far into the mountains. As we chatted they offered their bamboo hash pipe, wide and thick. Sucking, blowing and timing were the key to a successful smoke but as a novice I ended up coughing and spluttering. My guide was extremely unhappy at such goings on and promptly hauled me away, muttering under his breath about police and prison.

As we continued I realised we had not seen any machines on the mountain. We met donkey caravans loaded with goods, picking their way up the trail; a red-haired fellow Scot, as fair-skinned as I was, was having a battle with the sun. He had no sun cream and his face was red as a beetroot and peeling fast. His companion, an Australian, had enteric fever, his ribs protruding through his skin. After staying in Kathmandu for several weeks they had decided to trek but were now running out of money. It was at times like these that I felt quite ashamed of Westerners. The Nepalese are very hospitable and friendly but extremely poor and these visitors were contributing practically nothing to the country where they were guests. Moving along, there was a European male lying on the ground in the hot sun, an open umbrella by his side. Ang Kami, who had had enough of sick Westerners, would not stop. I managed to loosen the man's collar and ascertain he was still breathing before catching up with the team.

We eventually returned to the Pokhara Valley, to the strains of Cookie and Palu singing as they anticipated jingling some well-earned money in their pockets. I had a sneaking suspicion that Cookie was slightly inebriated on the way back as he was walking slower. We pitched camp by the lake, not anticipating the weather. I was about to settle into my sleeping bag when, with a whoosh, my tent was torn asunder and I was fully exposed to the elements. Amid fierce wind and torrential rain, heads down we scarpered to the nearest hotel. I managed to procure a seedy room that resembled a horse stall and where I spent a most uncomfortable night in the company of various insects. In the morning a light plane attempted to land on the airstrip while workmen chased a herd of cattle off it. Ang Kami joined me for breakfast in the hotel and then my excellent team caught the bus to Kathmandu where I thanked them, paid and parted company.

I spent the final day investigating a place called Freak Street, which a friend had told me about. It was so named because of the Europeans who lived there. They wore strange clothes, and existed on US$1 per day. I had to see it for myself. I changed my appearance, combing out my hair, washing off make-up and climbing into a pair of tatty jeans and grubby t-shirt. When I arrived I was unsure which building to enter so stood on the street and waited until I saw a European emerge from a doorway. I entered, walked along a dark passageway into a dimly-lit reception hall and asked to be shown a single room. It cost Rs.8, which at that time was half a US dollar. The room consisted of a double bed that could sleep several people, space for another two on the floor, and filthy blankets. Pretending to be a future tenant, I was told that a loaf of bread was one rupee, milk one rupee 60. Assuming that three or four people shared one room, it would be quite easy to exist on US$1.00 per day. The room was separated from others by a thin wall of plywood. On hearing voices, I knocked and entered. There were half a dozen men and women lying around smoking hash. The toilets had swinging half-doors resembling horse stalls and no hot water. I thanked the receptionist, declined the room and left, feeling quite depressed. What a waste of life and an insult to the Nepalese.

When I returned to the Nook hotel it was dark, the streets were crowded with young people running hither and thither in a panic, shouting and carrying torches. Evidently these were student riots demanding university places for poor families. Looking out the hotel window the next morning I saw police equipped with rifles surrounding the hotel. It was time to pack my bags.

The End

A DIET WITH A DIFFERENCE

I stepped off the plane in Tibet, zipped up my padded jacket, which was two sizes larger than normal due to my being over-weight and, carrying my rucksack, I caught the rickety old bus into the city. On reaching Lhasa, I set off to find lodgings. It was now mid-afternoon, and I was starving. (I had forgotten to book a vegetarian meal on the plane and therefore had received only sympathy from the air-hostess.)

Clutching my current Bible – a Mandarin phrasebook – I entered the yard of the Yak hotel and checked out my allocated space in a stone-floored room of four iron cots, with broken springs waving their antennae in the Arctic air. One cot held a youth of indeterminate age, sex and race, while in the corner were four chipped enamel basins with no running water.

Next, I inspected the loo to which my nose had unerringly led me. I peered over a low wall in the courtyard and saw three black holes for ladies and four for men. Sexism was alive and well in the Himalayas. Holding my breath, I retreated. This was not my bowl of rice. Leaving the hotel I trudged around Lhasa, my lungs heaving in the high altitude. Feeling light-headed, I finally located another lodging house where investi-gation revealed more upmarket facilities: two cots and no youth.

By this time I was dizzy from lack of oxygen and food. My stomach sucking voraciously at my spine, I dropped my heavy rucksack on the floor and went in search of sustenance. At an eating-house I pointed to the relevant phrases in my book and was eventually rewarded with a bowl of succulent, steaming, mouth-watering noodles. Chopsticks dancing in desperate fingers, I shifted the noodles in a very short space of time. Outside, several Tibetans clothed in robes of various styles and hue were chanting and twirling prayer wheels.

The lofty Himalayas, peaked in frozen silver, swept majestically above the city. The setting sun shone on the golden cupolas of the Dalai Lama, the Tibetan God-King in exile, the last forlorn hope of a forgotten people.

Later as dusk fell I walked through the market place surrounded by smells, chanting lamas, yaks, donkeys, sheep, goats and guttering candles and in a mood of exquisite anticipation of the coming day – a state of euphoria soon dispelled. On reaching my room I surrendered to a feeling of nausea and collapsed on to the shaky cot for the next 14 hours, rising at intervals only to vomit into the basin.

Despite my efforts to ignore it, daylight crept in through the ragged curtain, clear, bright and chilly. I eventually abandoned my cot and made my way slowly to the Potala, where I crawled up the seemingly endless broad steps, and finally stumbled into the fascinating, dim interior. My eyes adjusted to probe the corners of this haven of peace and Buddhism, but my empty stomach heaved and my nostrils twitched in recognition. Seeking the source of my queasiness I entered a vast, candle-lit, incense-laden temple where the echo of gongs boomeranged around the room. Massive golden images of ancient

Buddhas rested yoga-like in shadowy recesses. Flames writhed and squirmed as burgundy-robed lamas lit candles swimming in great vats of yak butter oil. My nostrils twitched again, and my stomach heaved once more as I realized what my bowl of noodles had been cooked in. I vowed to never again look the length of a noodle.

The following day, disenchanted with restaurants and with my jacket hanging from my now skeletal frame, I hired a bicycle and set off in the general direction of Kathmandu. As I cycled I purposefully averted my gaze from a billboard advertising Double Llama Cheese Cake. Grubby, weak starving but acclimatised, I pedalled off into the Himalayas.

The End

KASHMIR AND LADAKH

My lust for travel remained and I decided to visit Ladakh. I was teaching in the Vietnamese refugee camp in Hong Kong for those who had escaped the war in Vietnam. The teachers were of varying nationalities and included Kent, an Australian and Wendy, an American, who both expressed a desire to go.

We bought down jackets, sleeping bags and warm underwear in the Chinese emporium. After agreeing a date for leaving, and having obtained the necessary visas we met up at Kai Tak airport in Kowloon to board an Air India flight and celebrate with Champagne. We flew into Delhi and made our way to the Y.M.C.A.by taxi. On our first day we explored the Red Fort and the Chandri Chowk bazaar. The Red Fort is a muted red-brick building built in 1857, where Shah Jahan, a Mughal emperor, held court. It now sits in the centre of Delhi and is a huge visitor attraction. Chandri Chowk is a bustling market with many fascinating stalls and shops. The stall owners are friendly and there is an amazing variety of sundry goods, jewellery, colourful silks and saris and cloth adorned with tiny mirrors. To wander through the market is a delight with friendly, smiling salesmen on hand.

We had decided to spend our time in Kashmir on a houseboat, but did not know how to find one. Luckily, while collecting our backpacks at the airport we met Robert, an American, who asked if we would like to share a houseboat with him. He had previously lived on one and was familiar with the procedure. The weather was very cold but buds were already appearing on the branches of numerous trees along the way. The houses were large and tall; similar to those I had seen in Europe and built to house cattle and fodder in the winter. We alighted at the tourist centre and on exiting were met by a barrage of Kashmiris each vying to be our guide. We declined all offers and followed Robert down the road, accompanied by some of the men. As we walked I observed that some had amber eyes, others blue. They were dark-haired and handsome with straight, aquiline noses and wide smiles, and wore loose trousers with a long dark-tan cloak .

Snow lay on the mountaintops. Srinigar seemed to be a jumble of old wooden buildings interspersed with modern. The road ran alongside Dal Lake and we stopped at the steps where several *shikaras* were tied up. These are shallow wooden boats with a canopy and comfortable seating on which to recline while the boatman, who sits at the back, paddles out to the houseboat of one's choice. Robert asked passing boatmen if they knew of Ahmed and his houseboat *The Violet*. The grapevine at work soon presented Ahmed's *shikara* heading toward us. We let Robert argue and finally agree a price of a very few pounds for our stay on the boat. We joined Ahmed in his *shikara* and he paddled through a maze of boats to *The Violet*, where his family waited to greet us and welcome us on board.

Wooden steps led to a veranda opening into a comfortably furnished room with sofas, coffee tables and fitted carpet. From there a short passage led to two rooms, one each for the men, while Wendy and I had a room with en suite and two single beds at the stern. Living on a houseboat means being taken into the bosom of the family, who take very good care of their guests, providing everything possible to make life comfortable. The family live and sleep on a houseboat nearby, from where meals are provided. Drinking water is supplied from a different lake as Dal Lake is polluted and seaweed grows near the surface. As the weather was cold stoves were lit and warmed the rooms. Very cosy. Sitting on the veranda was a unique experience. Flat-bottomed boats appeared, and a thriving trade operated from them, selling soft drinks, colourful, hand-woven shawls, silver ornaments, jewellery, fruit and other goods too numerous to mention. The boatmen were always good-humoured, even when one declined their goods so I felt obliged to be the same.

The next morning we sat around the dining table consuming eggs, tea and toast and discussing how to spend the day. We decided to go our separate ways. Visiting the market, I purchased a military-style khaki sweater, long, woollen military socks and rubber boots. All the clothes seemed to be military and I wondered if they had been purchased from a barracks. I asked the shopkeeper, a large man wearing a turban and cloak, if he would buy them back when I returned, to which he agreed. I then hired a bicycle to ride around and explore some of the town, before returning to *The Violet* and leaving the bicycle to be picked up at the steps, as agreed. The next day, we planned to visit the airport to book seats for Leh, capital of Lladakh.

We reserved seats for Wednesday, two days hence. Flying to Ladakh could be problematic as we found out whilst trying to get a booking. We were allocated seats 127, 128 and 129 and informed that there were only 80 seats on the plane; we would be on the waiting list and should turn up in case there was a vacancy. When the clerk saw my disbelief, he repeated the advice. Sixty seats were reserved for the military (we found out later) in case of trouble in Ladakh, which is a very sensitive area. The Chinese have taken control of the north of Ladakh, and India is ensuring that they do not encroach further. The area surrounding Leh and further afield, had established military camps, both Indian and Chinese.

Since we had a couple of days to wait, Mahomet the family's guide, led us to the bus station. We wished to visit Pahalgam, which was a good distance away, situated at the foot of the snow-capped Himalayas. At Pahalgam we examined the interior of several hotels until, satisfied, we chose The Woodstock. Once settled, the cold was so intense that we curled up in our sleeping bags, piled blankets on top and fell asleep.

The next day after a breakfast of toast and tea, I went for a walk. The towering mountainside was covered in pine trees and wooden chalets, sitting on the hillsides clothed in white, waiting for the melting snow and the tourist season to begin. Wandering around the shops I met the locals who all wore the long, blanket-like capes seen in Srinigar called *pharangs*. Each person, men and women alike, looked pregnant and I could not understand why. Entering a shop the assistant produced something from under her *pharang* and carefully handed it to me. Mystery solved. The object, shaped like a flowerpot and made of clay, contained burning charcoal and sat within in a basket. This ingenious item was called a *khungri* and it was clutched beneath the *pharang*. It was certainly effective as the heat was intense. As I left the shop, I handed it back reluctantly – thinking how very handy it would be in Scotland.

I am unable to resist hills and strolled up the nearest one. But it was so wet underfoot that my feet sank into the snow and soon I abandoned the idea. Just then a young lad appeared leading two ponies, which seemed a more exciting way of getting around. Although I was unfamiliar with horses I hired one and rode unsteadily back to the Woodstock, where Wendy and Kent and I decided to catch the bus back to Srinagar to escape the wet.

Cows, sheep and goats milled around the many villages we passed. Houses were mainly three storeys with sloping roofs. We arrived at the houseboat to a meal served by Hamid, the family's chief cook and bottle-washer.

Wednesday. Time to leave for the airport to find out if we had a flight to Leh. We were rather worried as we had anticipated seats might not be available for us. Thankfully, on arrival, we had seats. The military must have been having a quiet day. Airport security was very thorough. The officer who searched my bag found a small penknife and held it up triumphantly in my face, as if to say: 'you thought you would smuggle this in?' To tell the truth I had forgotten it was there, in the bottom of my bag. The other customs' I had passed through at different airports had not found it; this man was efficient. He said I could not keep it with me, but could retrieve it from the pilot on landing.

Meanwhile, Wendy had wandered on to the tarmac with her camera and was gaily snapping away until three large soldiers appeared and escorted her into a room to confiscate the film. Kent and I were already boarding and fortunately Wendy joined us, shaken but otherwise unharmed. The scenery was breath-taking. We flew straight over the mighty Himalayas whose snow-capped peaks jutted into the sky in all their white-clad glory. We peered out of the windows in awe of such splendour and grandeur.

In 1982 Leh airport consisted of two huts from one of which we collected our baggage and my knife. On exiting we were approached by two ladies dressed in native costume who assured us they had a very good hotel and persuaded us to accompany them. With no notion of where to stay we were happy to follow them.

We piled into a Jeep and drove to a hotel, aptly named the Khungri. For Rs. 25 we could have a single room each, with bathroom but no running water as the pipes were frozen. Hot water would be delivered in the morning and, after that, only cold water would be available. The electricity worked occasionally, but went off at 11.30 p.m. Leh had one main street of shops and restaurants. The scenery was flat, brown and dusty, surrounded by hills, not a green shoot in sight. The Indus river wound its way through the parched earth and on through the town. The fields, which were surrounded by dykes, contained no crops but were well irrigated nonetheless. This was winter and not the tourist season. The days were sunny and slightly warmer than the very cold nights. Tibetans and Ladakis lived side-by-side and I admired their colourful costumes and odd-shaped hats.

Once settled, Kent and I caught a bus to Tiskey Gompa and Lamasery. We ascended the steps, puffing and panting in the thin air. Inside, empty prayer stools awaited the lamas, statues peered from shelves and tantras of many hues hung from the ceiling. A shiver ran down my spine as I thought of the ancient traditions that lay behind this. We came out of the dark into sunshine. There were no buses so we started to walk. Perspiring profusely we removed our parkas and, freezing, put them back on. Fortunately a military Jeep came by and we hitched a ride with the Indian officer, who told us that after two years in Ladakh he was still not used to the lack of oxygen. The soldiers lived in a cantonment, several of which were scattered around the barren land, miles away from town. We were invited to spend time there but declined. I silently wondered if there was any hot water in the area.

Next day we went to the airport to book a seat for the return journey, bearing in mind we might not get one for some days. (We had been refused a return ticket at Srinagar because of the military quota.) Here we met Kelam, the man in charge of the airport, who ensured that we got tickets but without any guarantee of a seat. He invited us to dinner that evening. We gratefully accepted – food was scarce in Leh. Supplies came by air, but since there was only one flight daily and the plane could not fly in inclement weather, food was short in winter.

Breakfasts consisted of tea and dry biscuits, lunches and dinners of noodles. In the dining room we were consistently handed extensive menus and on our first day we had drooled over the variety of fare listed. However, each item we ordered was off the menu.

We arrived at Kelam's house that night. He lit the stove and, as the electricity had broken down, the candles too. He employed a very good cook who served a delicious meal. Presumably the food had been flown in by special request, as it was not available in town.

It was a stone-built house with bare floor boards in the dining-cum-living room, a bed and some chairs. We chatted until midnight, when it was time to return to the hotel and Kelam kindly supplied us with a torch as there were no streetlights, but the stars were bright and it was a cloudless sky, so we managed. We crept along the silent alleyways to discover the great, wooden doors surrounding the garden of the hotel locked. I did not wish to shout and cause a disturbance, so found a foothold and climbed over, waiting for the others to join me. Just then there was a snarling and growling at my feet--I had forgotten about the dogs. Fortunately, Wendy appeared and since she had made a point of befriending the animals earlier, they quietened down. This night out was the only form of nightlife we had.

The next day I decided to go on a pony trek to Stok and went in search of the stables. I was invited into the owner's house to meet his family. A dark-haired child gazed in wonder from behind its mother's skirt while she was busy making tea for the Memsahib. As there were no chairs, we sat on the bed covered with beautiful, hand-woven rugs. It was not actually a bed but a long, wooden bench fixed to the wall and used as occasion demanded. While sipping tea we bargained amicably before settling on a price. Accompanied by the owner, I mounted my pony and we trotted down the street together. I noticed that the roofs of the houses were used for drying and storing fodder. The animals, *dzos* (half-yak, half-cow) goats, sheep and ponies, grazed at the side of the road, although there was not much foliage. My pony was frisky and I suspected it was the first ride of the season, as it slipped and bucked on the wet surface. As I was not used to horses I could barely manage.

Stok lay in the foothills of a barren area of land, with snow-topped mountains disappearing into the horizon. I inquired about trekking further but the high passes were blocked with heavy snowfalls. Most of the houses were whitewashed huts; the people were friendly. However, there were many dogs that scared me as they milled around my pony. Perhaps they did not like the smell of strangers? Returning to the hotel I found Wendy in bed with hypothermia, which I eventually succumbed to. We remained in our day clothes and snuggled into sleeping bags on which our hostesses piled blankets and filled hot water bottles for us throughout the day. We thought we would never be warm again. We had been dashing around since we arrived and had not become acclimatised to the lack of oxygen.

Later that week we took the bus to Saboo, a little village in the hills where there was to be an archery contest.

A low, colourful tent resembling a marquee was set out on the arid land where no other buildings existed. Inside, the ground was covered in beautiful, hand-woven carpets on top of which were small yellow, orange and brown-painted tables. Behind each one sat a contestant observing his opponents firing their bows. In front of each man a small cup was constantly filled with tea from very large kettles. While travelling in Ladakh and Tibet it behoves one to carry a wooden bowl for tea as no cup, no tea. Utensils were scarce. After a while Kent and I wandered into the hills, over boulders and barren land. Reaching the top of one hill we felt the urge to discover what lay beyond but eventually the monotony of the scenery drove us back to the contest. We later discovered there were 150 miles of hills!

We thoroughly enjoyed the friendliness extended to us: the colour, excitement and competitive games but hunger overtook us; we had not brought a picnic or utensils and so decided to return to the hotel. There we met two young Australians:

Steve, an ornithologist and zoologist and Peter, a geologist. They had come to Leh on a quest: to find a snow leopard and take rock samples. They told us they were planning to ride deep into the Himalayas in a Jeep the next day. We wanted to visit the remote Lamayuru Monastery that lay in the same direction, so five of us set off with a driver at the crack of dawn the following day.

Our personal geologist explained the rock formation and ever-changing colours, making it a very interesting journey. Five hours later, feeling dizzy from the switchback road that snaked its way along the foot of the mountains following the course of the river, we arrived. Steve and Peter, having asked the driver to wait, strode off into the mountains. Kent, Wendy and I entered the monastery, which was situated in the middle of the village, where young lads, training to be lamas, lived. The older lamas were friendly, gave us a conducted tour, and we were invited for tea. Concerned by the fact we had no cups or bowls, a lad was sent off to find some. He returned with dirty glasses that were washed out with tea and then filled from a huge kettle.

We sipped and chatted and chatted and sipped, trying not to look at each other, as to how well we were coping with this butter tea, which was definitely an acquired taste. The problem was, that after each sip, the glass was filled again, until the enormous kettle was empty. Fortunately, the lamas enjoyed their tea immensely, hence the large kettle, so barely noticed our reaction. We managed to leave without losing face. The young boys, who had been taken in to study at the lamasery, had shaven heads and wore dark-brown robes.

On returning to the Jeep we saw Steve holding a plastic bag, which contained some droppings he thought were from elusive snow leopards.

Steve showed us hair, teeth and bones of a small animal which had been devoured, and which he was taking back to Australia to study. I often wonder how he managed to pass through customs with it. Peter had managed to collect rock samples, so we were all satisfied with our successful trip into the interior. The Jeep once more followed the rugged contour of the Himalayas as we returned to the hotel.

The next day Ladakhi ladies were seen at street corners, laying out carrots and potatoes in small piles on the road. We sighed in relief at the thought of a change of diet. Our relief from noodles was supplied by a couple, Joan and Henry, who arrived after us and had brought some cheese with them. To celebrate Easter day, at breakfast Joan very generously and carefully cut five small slices of cheese. Never had cheese tasted so good. Now it was nearing time to leave so I wanted a souvenir of the country. I walked around the few shops on the street until I espied a small, silver, cylindrical container holding wooden chopsticks and a knife. Carried at the waist, this object is used by Tibetans and Ladakhis as they travel, enabling hospitable housewives to offer sustenance. When told the price I discovered, to my dismay, that I did not have enough rupees, and so bargained with the owner who accepted a packet of Rothman's cigarettes in exchange.

Time to leave and we packed our rucksacks, saying a fond farewell to our hostesses. We had been well looked after. We arrived at the airport by Jeep and joined the queue for a seat on the plane. As before, seats were reserved for the military and there were too many passengers. After a very long, cold wait we spotted Kelam, who kindly detached us from the queue and gave us reserved seats. Without his aid we might have been in Ladakh for some time longer than anticipated, so we were very grateful.

We once again flew over breath-taking scenery; the sunlight glinting on the white tips of the mountains below as the plane dipped and dived in the turbulent air then, steadying, to swoop to a perfect landing at Srinagar – where we ran into trouble. We had boarded the airport bus that, as we neared the town, was stopped by the police who told us to stay in our seats; there were riots in town and it was dangerous to go further. Then they disappeared, leaving us frustrated, cold and tired. Eventually, a group of police arrived and, like sheep, we followed them across the bridge leading into town. As we crossed I saw Mahomet on the other side, keeping pace with us. I waved and ran across to talk to him at which point one officer ran after me and, with baton swinging, herded me back into the group. Kashmir is disputed territory: India and Pakistan both claim it thus riots were frequent.

We arrived at the tourist centre, 20 hungry tired and dishevelled travellers. The officer wanted us to stay the night there, however, one glance at the cold stone floor and I asked him politely if I could leave. He yelled at me and told me not to be stupid. I backed off but, five minutes later, tried again. This time, his face suffused in red, I watched, fascinated, as his moustache jumped up and down in time with his shout. Finally he gave in if I had a place to go, but he would not be responsible for my safety. I thanked him and, with a nod to Mahomet, picked up my rucksack and walked out. As I did so, I noticed Kent, Wendy, Steve, Peter, a French couple and two Germans following. The officer had washed his hands of everyone. Mahomet organised us into *shikaris* and we were paddled to *The Violet*. I wondered where we would all be accommodated but the family coped well – nothing seemed too much trouble. We three slept in our own rooms and the others found a place for their sleeping bags on the lounge floor.

The next day dawned bright and clear. After breakfast, I hailed a passing *shikara* and then a scooter, which took me to Lal Chowk to return the clothes I had bought for Leh. As I sat down a policeman promptly jumped in and accompanied me all the way to the market. He was looking after the tourists. The shop was closed and I was advised that all Muslim shops were closed that day. The scooter then took the policeman and I back to the shops by the lake. I wanted to buy a Kashmir rug in one of the many beautiful carpet shops that lined the street. The officer, seeing me safely ensconced in the shop, took his leave. I wandered around admiring gorgeous carpets and rugs, followed by the owner who explained the colours and patterns. They were all rolled up, underside exposed, so that the customer could see how well-crafted they were, as the pattern was the same on both sides. When I spied the rug I wanted, I sat down cross-legged on the floor and pointed to my choice. The shopkeeper, however, insisted that I saw them all unrolled. Tea was served and I watched as his assistants threw down rug after rug. I was then asked to choose. I pointed to the first one, paid, rolled it up and caught a *shikara* back to the boat. It had been an entertaining day but still my winter clothes were tucked under my arm. I eventually left them with Ahmed's family.

In the evening after dinner we enjoyed the company of the different nationalities on board. Our stay had been very comfortable; the family had been wonderful but the riots on the street continued and being confined was not what we had intended. It was time to return to Delhi. We said goodbye to the others who seemed content to wait out the troubles and, with Mahomet as our guard, we joined a luxury coach to Jammu. We sank wearily into the comfortable seats, looking forward to sleep. Alas, this was not to be. A television, blaring out Indian music accompanied by erotic dancing, assailed us most of the way. When we arrived at Jammu we had no time to explore and instead waited in the tourist reception centre for our coach to Delhi.

The hilly, winding road was crawling with military vehicles, revealing the unrest in the area. Ten hours later, tired and hungry, we arrived at Delhi, took a taxi to the Y.M.C.A. to rest and pick up our suitcases for our onward journey to Dharamsala. I hoped to meet His Holiness, the Dalai Lama who now lived there.

The End

THE DUSTY ROAD TO DHARAMSALA

Kent, Wendy and I left the Delhi Y.M.C.A. at 6.30. a.m. and caught a taxi to the local bus station, where we were to leave for Dharamsala that morning.

The bus depot was busy and noisy. Dozens of buses were lined up, awaiting passengers and emitting black smoke from exhausts, creating a dense fug. Men in dhotis clambered onto the bus roofs, to secure sacks of rice, cages of clucking hens, and various boxes of goods including television sets. They were directed by sari-clad ladies wearing golden nose rings and a red temple dot on the forehead while husbands ushered the children on board.

Prior to climbing on board we asked several drivers which was our bus because, in my experience, it took five answers to get the right one. As we boarded we noticed that the bus was gaily bedecked with fancy idols dancing in the windscreen, obscuring the driver's view. A riot of gay patterns adorned the side panelling. Then a fierce revving of engines amid clouds of dark smoke sent us on our way.

An early morning mist hovered over the dusty streets as we sped onto the open highway. The sun rose in a blaze of red, and shone on water-logged paddy fields. Water buffaloes stood in the shallows, grey hides glistening, oblivious to passing traffic as they chewed the cud, their great heads resting contentedly on the surface of the water. Village ladies with water urns balanced on their heads looked resplendent in the golds, reds, blues and silver of their native dress as they glided sedately through the high, dry grass, one behind the other. Another day's work lay ahead: pounding spices, cooking, swilling out and cleaning the cooking pots and caring for children.

On we travelled along the two-way highway, amid dust thrown up from passing vehicles –lopsidedly-laden trucks with horns blaring, drivers' elbows jutting out of window-less door –our driver's assistant hung half out of the passenger door, spitting betel nut, banging and shouting to ensure his driver missed the oncoming traffic and to keep the bus on the straight-and-narrow, despite the dust that covered the windscreen. Then, suddenly, a bone-racking shudder as the bus came to a standstill beside a road hut.

'Chai stop, twenty minutes', he shouted in Hindi and English. We tumbled out to partake of the sustenance that would help us endure the hot, humid and dusty 12-hour journey into the Himalayas. Engulfed by the delicious aroma of exotic spices we raced to find a seat. Only minutes later, a horn sounded and then another. Since all the buses stopped at these chai stops, we had no idea which one was ours. Fortunately our driver sent one of the passengers to fetch us when he saw we were missing. How well we were looked after in India. We stopped every two hours for chai (tea) and food, both to give the two drivers a rest and for us to eat.

Weary, hungry and dusty, we arrived in the gathering dusk. Our cases were unloaded from the roof and piled on the road with all the other baggage. As I picked mine up a young Tibetan man approached. Lightly built, he had deep-brown eyes, smooth skin and heightened cheekbones. He asked if I was a teacher, to which I replied in the affirmative. He introduced himself as Thupten Tsering Lee. Thupten offered to show me around in exchange for practising his English. This was an opportunity not to be missed. I introduced him to Wendy and Kent and asked if he could recommend a hotel.

We settled for the Tibet Hotel. Since it was cheap at Rs. 30 per night Wendy and I decided to have the luxury of a room each. The rooms were en suite, with an Asian toilet and cold water. Thupten left us, promising to return after breakfast. For dinner we had a spicy meat dish with rice. In the evening I went for a walk. The night was dark and the stars shone and twinkled. I was able to pick out the most common constellations: the Plough and the Seven Sisters.

The next day dawned bright, clear and hot. Thupten arrived and we caught a bus to McLeod Ganj and discovered a church, St. John's in the Wilderness, standing in its own grounds. Walking around I noticed the grave of 'James Bruce - Lord Elgin, 1863', he of the Elgin marbles. Afterwards we went for lunch in the Om restaurant. The masala tea was delicious and boiled with spices and milk. Afterwards we went to a Tibetan drama – *The Monkey's Paw* – an adaptation of an English drama. At night, there was a disco and dancing to strobe lighting in a wooden shed. We met many young Tibetans who had traversed the secret passage through the mountains from Tibet. The young stayed in Dharamsala for their education; the older ones went to college in the south.

Thupten was studying to be a Tibetan herbal doctor and worked in the medical centre. During the summer, the students trekked into the mountains with donkeys, and picked the herbs the doctors needed. At the centre these were sifted in an old-fashioned riddle and shaken to take out the stones and weeds. I was fascinated with this seemingly primitive method and decided to make an appointment with the doctor as my curiosity got the better of me. The lady doctor was very thorough in her examination and finally, after taking my pulse, diagnosed anaemia. I was given a round, brown pill about the size of my pinky nail which was wrapped in blue ribbon and tied with red cotton.

The next day, Kent and Wendy took the bus to the hill station at Manali. I decided to climb the mountain just behind Dharamsala. I was not at that time aware of the size of the mountain – it was just there and I loved walking. At one point I met a wizened man of the hills coming down. He indicated to me to sit on a rock beside him, patting his thighs to show his pain. I produced two oranges and we consumed them in companionable silence before separating. I climbed to the tree line and sat down for a rest. I thought I detected a shuffling and sat against a tree trunk so that my back was covered. Were there bears here? I had forgotten to ask about wild animals. I took out my puny pocket-knife and stuck it in the ground in front of me to await events. Nothing appeared. I drank some water from my rucksack, ate a cereal bar, withdrew my knife and continued on my way.

As I climbed thatched cottages appeared just below the top of the mountain. It had been a steep, tough walk up and I was now thirsty and tired. A woman was standing, watching me. I put my hands together and namaste'd, asking for panni (water) which she very kindly fetched. I then made my way along to the other, seemingly empty cottages and walking into one, I was startled to hear a deep voice. When my eyes adjusted to the dark, I saw a young man in his late twenties with blond hair and blue eyes lying on the floor. Niels had come to see the Dalai Lama but so far had been unsuccessful. One day, while hill walking, he had discovered this vacant cottage and decided to stay a week and commune with nature. I declined the offer to stay the night, and walked on, intending to return the way I had come, but got totally lost. At one point, unable to see a way down the mountain, I walked forward to the very edge of a cliff. Back-tracking rapidly I went in the other direction. There was no easy way down but taking what I thought was the simplest route, I peered over the side of the slope and started my descent, slipping and sliding and grabbing branches to stop me from falling.

Fortunately my trainers gave a very good grip on the slippery rock. I was dressed in long-sleeved T-shirt and long trousers with a hat, but even so, the sun cream proved ineffective in protecting my fair skin. Nearing the base I looked around and in the distance on the side of the mountain saw movement. Men were working the slate, moving it in wheelbarrows. I must have looked a sight as they immediately came to help, sat me down in the shade of a makeshift corrugated iron roof, gave me water and would not let me move. I could feel my face as red as beetroot and this must have alarmed them. After half an hour, one of them indicated that I should traverse the mountain in the direction of the next group of workers. On reaching them I was put in a wheelbarrow and passed on to the next and last group who ensured that I was walking towards the town. I was extremely grateful to these men for rescuing me and thanked them profusely, at which they just grinned and muttered 'Memsahib'. At the hotel I had a cold shower and fell into bed.

The following day, my two companions, who had returned from their trip, left by bus for Delhi and Bangkok. I waved them goodbye and not forgetting I had come in the hope of meeting the Dalai Lama, went to the relevant office with my request – only to be turned down. Thupten and I had dinner that night: lots of different noodles, *mo mo* (dumplings) and rice, and then he mentioned he would ask if I could meet the Dalai Lama. This he did, and the next day I joined the line waiting to greet him. I was told that to present him with a white scarf was traditional, and duly bought one. The 'Palace' is a large bungalow in its own grounds, so he has privacy. Tibetans were the first in line and as they moved forward some bowed, others prostrated. When my turn came, I presented him with the scarf and he shook my hand. We had a short conversation in which he asked where I was from. I felt as if I was in a great presence and tears flooded my eyes.

I met Europeans robed in burgundy, the women with shaven heads. They were staying to study Buddhist teachings. They were a happy group, very friendly, laughing and smiling as they came out of their studies.

The next day I attempted to climb a different mountain. However, having walked only a few paces, a hill man who was descending stood in front of me, gesturing to turn back. When I looked at him enquiringly he pointed to the sky and imitated rain. The weather was fine–though humid – but an hour later and back at the hotel, the heavens opened and thunder rolled around the town.

The following day, Thupten took a half-day off work and we walked to Forsythe Ganj where his teacher from South India had arrived to consult a doctor. Thupten wanted to renew his acquaintance. We entered a cottage and the lady of the house asked us to sit down on the padded divan seat placed against the wall. She did not speak English and neither of the men sharing the divan did either, so Thupten translated. There were six other men including the teacher, who was quite small and reminded me of Gandhi. He was clad in a robe, his demeanour marking him out as someone of standing. He was quietly spoken and gracious. He told the story of past Dalai Lamas, how they had come to be chosen, how they had been revered. He finished by saying the prediction was that the fourteenth Dalai Lama, that is the present one, would be the last. Thinking on the past events of recent years this would certainly make sense.

The lady of the house had handed each of us a large glass and poured the contents of a very big kettle into it, which I thought was tea. I took a sip and nearly choked – it turned out to be *chang* (the local brew made from barley). Unfortunately for me, she was such a good hostess that she immediately refilled my glass, and not to drink was a mark of disrespect. The room was lit by oil lamps, the atmosphere spiritual, otherworldly. We were transported from the modern world to another, mystical one in a mountainous country, where peace reigned and Buddhism played a large part in the daily life of its people. When the teacher finished his story, the Tibetans talked amongst themselves and I sat and listened, appreciating that I had been accepted into their way of life, albeit for a short time. Thupten said goodbye to his old teacher, thanked our hostess (who was the teacher's daughter) and we stumbled into the darkness. There were no lights. Only the stars and moon lit the way as we walked back. It was a very satisfying evening, although I was more than a little tipsy.

The next day I washed my clothes in the river and laid them out on the rocks to dry. Long- haired, curious goats wandered over to inspect me as I lay basking in the sun. I had acquired a taste for the local brew and sipped at a bottle.

It was nearing my time to leave and I wanted to buy a rug as a souvenir of my stay. There were no carpet shops in this rather remote area but one day when I was shopping a shop-keeper had admired my parka and I had admired the rug on the shop floor. When I mentioned this to Thupten, he said that the man might bargain because it was difficult to get good, warm clothing. We walked into the shop and the two men held a conversation about the price. Although the shop-keeper was keen to bargain, my parka was not enough to exchange for the rug, so I also offered my rucksack, a carton of English cigarettes – a great bargaining chip – and a Rs.100. Deal done. I became the proud owner of a beautiful, thick Tibetan rug with an indigo background and red and yellow designs – unique. At the hotel, I rolled up the rug and Thupten acquired a sack and sewing kit from the receptionist, which he used to wrap it up for my journey home. That night I said farewell to all the friendly people I had met. I promised to keep in touch, especially with my young friend, and wished him luck in his studies to become a Tibetan doctor.

At 6 a.m. the next morning, my rug and suitcase were stowed on the roof of the bus along with the other passengers' luggage, and we set off for the long, dusty, noisy journey back to Delhi and a flight home.

The End

DARJEELING

In the hot summers of India my mother would have taken the family to the hill station of Darjeeling. Now I wanted to visit. I flew to Bogdugra, the tiny airport in the North. My passport was stamped and I exited into a street crowded with excited children.

Expecting local transport I was disappointed to find there was only one tourist bus that was quickly filling up with children on their way back to boarding school after the holidays. I hired a taxi but soon realised they were not for the sole use of one passenger, and so we were five. After agreeing a fare, we set off. Sharing the car were a married couple, two young lads and myself as we began the hair-raising four-hour ride into the Himalayas.

The scenery was fascinating. On our way we passed tea plantations and the toy train, chugging and wending its way up the mountains which would arrive in Darjeeling 9 hours after setting off with a full complement of passengers. The train is a throwback to the days of the Raj in colonial India, when Memsahibs took to the cool hill stations, to escape the shattering heat of an Indian summer on the plains. We drove past Hindu Temples and Tibetan shrines to arrive in Darjeeling before the train. This town appears to be hanging on the mountainside, with twisting roads winding in and out of the rows of houses, which are perched on the hillsides. My hotel, the Planters Club, was a long low construction, with a wooden veranda running its length, and a view looking down across houses to distant mountains. The town was rather quaint, small shops selling souvenirs, Indian silver, Tibetan ornaments, colourful Bhutanese bags and Darjeeling tea. It seethed with Tibetan refugees, having fled their country after the Chinese invasion, and the escape of the Dalai Lama, their God-King, in 1959. Some made their living by hiring out ponies or working the crafts they had acquired in Tibet. At night, the smoky atmosphere of burning incense and cooking fires permeated the mountain air. It was exhilarating.

The hotel had wooden floors, delightful small lounges opening on to the veranda and coal fires, which were a blessing as it was very chilly. I was greeted by flashing teeth and 'How are you Memsahib?' This was definitely an improvement on Mrs! I was shown to my upstairs room and was delighted to find another coal fire and a hot-water bottle. This was bliss. I did, however, have a mission to accomplish. Prior to setting off a friend had asked me to deliver a small parcel to her family who lived in the hills. Evidently there was only one telephone in their village and therefore patience was required. I was to learn a lot about patience in India. I duly managed to contact them and the sister invited me to visit their farm. She would send her Nepalese employee in the morning at 8.00 a.m. to guide me there. That settled, I wandered into the streets of Darjeeling. A procession of Nepalese men, women and children walked through the streets chanting, which added to the romantic atmosphere.

When darkness fell I was surrounded by a horde of young lads all offering to be my guide to Tiger Hill to view the top of

Kangchenjunga from a distance. The catch is that one rises at 4.00 a.m. in pitch darkness, to hang around shivering in the freezing mountain air until all the tourists arrive and, if the gods are willing, the clouds lift to reveal the mountains. The gods however, were not benevolent that day. I climbed back into the Jeep, looked reproachfully at Bemal, my young guide who had failed to mention that I might not see the mountain.

As compensation, we visited a Tibetan temple where my guide dotted my forehead with red powder and explained many of the customs. Back at the hotel for breakfast, the receptionist asked for my permit. 'To be here you need a permit' she told me. But here I was, without one. I was then instructed to report to the police station immediately. 'Yes, after breakfast and a cup of this delicious tea', I replied, having no intention of doing so. I was saved by a whistle and a 'Memsahib' sounded from below the window. 'I am from Meera; we must leave at once to catch the bus.'

Abandoning breakfast and any thoughts of the police I answered the call, picked up my bag and joined Nanjay – the delightful Nepalese who had come to lead me to the farm. Grabbing my hand-woven bag, he set off at a canter down the hill to the market. Down the winding streets, into back alleys, passing ponies, shops and stalls, pushing our way through throngs of people we eventually arrived at the crowded bus terminal just in time to catch the only bus for the next four hours to our destination. Leaping onto the bus amid shouts, flying chickens and bags of goods strewn across the floor, we finally found separate seats. Nanjay promptly fell asleep and I enjoyed observing the other passengers, trying to understand the lingo and gazing at the passing scenery. Over hill and dale, mountains and valleys, I saw women plucking tealeaves on the

hillsides, the plantations stretching into the distance surrounded by snowy mountain tops. With a finger on the horn,
accelerator pressed to the floor, the driver managed to pass
everything on that narrow road: cars, ponies, carts.

Two hours later when I was beginning to wonder if we had
missed the stop, Nanjay woke up as if programmed, looked
out of the window, and indicated to get off. I alighted thankfully, looking forward to a cup of tea, but it was not to be. I
was led to the foot of a very high hill where there nestled a tiny
village with two shops and a few wooden house-like structures.
Bullocks stood by a single tree in the village square; chickens
scratched the earth. Well, I thought, what happens now? I
was impatient as usual, but this was timeless India where
nothing is done in a hurry, not with all day to do it. I sank
down on the wooden steps of the nearest shop but the shop-
keeper quickly produced a rug for me to sit on. He handed me
a cup of tea and with a gap-toothed smile, sat down in a chair
perched precariously on the steps. I accepted the tea revolted
at the sight of two dirty cracks in the cup but smiled and
gulped it down before I changed my mind. I did not want to
be inhospitable in this very hospitable country. I produced a
packet of St Moritz cigarettes and handed them round. Nanjay,
the shopkeeper, the other shopkeeper, his friend across the
road, a passing villager and was that a 12-year-old boy? All
helped themselves. Smiling and nodding we sat together in a
friendly atmosphere.

After some time had passed my sturdy guide said, 'soon
now.' Well, I was unaware of what was going to happen soon
but it was getting rather hot and swarms of flies were buzzing
around. Perhaps smoking here was a necessity? I picked up my
cigarette pack from behind me to find only two cigarettes

remained. I looked up to see someone approaching with a horse. 'Up, memsahib', said my guide. I looked at him in astonishment but brooking no delay he set my foot in the stirrup, gave me a push into the saddle, took the bridle and without a backward glance at his charge, led the horse up the valley and into the hills. No buses here then.

Very soon we were climbing and had collected two followers. Up over the hills, past thatched cottages, huts dotted at intervals along the way with pigs squealing and chickens raking in the dried, dun coloured grass. Men and women appeared at doors along the path, shouting and waving as we went by. Up, over dusty paths, the horse picked its sure-footed way over the stones – which was just as well as there was nothing I could do to help.

Trees lined the way and after a time we stopped, tied the horse to a tree and, with Nanjay's help, I dismounted. Sore, I decided to stand, fishing another pack of cigarettes from my bag looped over the saddle. We had a smoke then re-mounted and set off. My guide was striding along. Poor fellow, I thought, walking for hours. Calling his attention, I indicated it was his turn to ride. With an engaging smile he shook his head and walked on. I hoped I had not insulted him. He must have thought me useless to know nothing about horses. I looked around from my lofty position, at the Nepalese, the two followers, the hills and, not far away, Sikkim. I felt like the Queen of Sheba waving to the villagers as we passed them. I was in a strange land, among strange people but not amongst strangers. Bursting into song, I treated all within earshot to 'I'll tak' the high road'. One hour later, picking our way through trees, we arrived at a thatched house. Leading the horse (I never did find out its name) to some steps, Nanjay helped me dismount once again. Our followers departed.

Soon a little girl and boy appeared, carefully carrying a glass of milk. This was nectar. Laughing and giggling they danced away. How I was being looked after! Another cigarette, back onto the horse and off we went. We soon arrived at the farm. It was a hive of activity. Workers were busily stacking hay, gathering spices to be marketed and cutting huge leaves off the trees. Meera, her mother and grandmother greeted me and offered their hospitality. The house had been built by Meera's great-grandfather who had built the farm up around it. It was a charming place, nestling in the hills. There were pigs, spices and a butter and cheese dairy. At night, oil lamps were lit which made it all seem quite romantic. After a delicious, spicy meal we chatted, bringing the women the latest news of their sister. We looked at photos-Meera had been to Budh Gaya the year before-and then we sipped *chang* served in a small barrel-shaped container inlaid with silver bands. This barrel was filled with millet seeds over which water was poured, and sipped through a straw. It was warm, tasted rather like a heavy port, was delicious and, I soon found out, quite potent. I gave Meera the vitamin pills entrusted to me and retired. Lighting my way by lamp, she warned me that I would have to be up early to return to Darjeeling – and so had no time to explore. I felt extremely privileged to have been able to visit the family.

I was awakened long after the sun had risen. After breakfast, with a wave and my thanks, it was with a sense of relief that we were now using Shanks' pony. Nanjay and I set off. Going downhill this time we ran, jumped muddy little streams and stopped to take photos by a Nepalese shrine. A few hours later we descended on to a road. This was the end of the journey for Nanjay. He stopped an approaching Jeep and bargained my fare to Darjeeling. We shook hands and this marvellous man smiled, nodded and disappeared back up the hill.

Musing at the staying power of the Nepalese, I climbed in with local passengers to settle down for the long drive back. The Jeep sped along rutted roads up winding hills, passed tea gardens to arrive in time for an evening meal just as dusk was falling. I retired early. A hot-water bottle had been put in my bed and a fire lit in my room. Bliss.

In the morning as I sat at the breakfast table enjoying toast, boiled egg and a lovely pot of tea, the receptionist joined me and asked for my permit. I told her that I had not yet visited the police station but would do so soon, though I knew that it was too late to get one and would permission have been granted had I applied in Calcutta, I wondered? She said that the intelligence agents had been looking for me the day before.

I finished breakfast, returned to my room and hastily packed my case, paid the bill and ran down the hill to the bus station. I was fortunate to catch the next bus to Siliguri, once more enduring a cacophony of clucking hens. I squeezed in beside sacks of rice and all the goods and chattels the other passengers had brought, thankful to have a seat.

The End

SOUTH INDIA

Perhaps because I was born in the Himalayas I had kept to the north of India, in the mountains and valleys. I now wanted to explore the south and booked an Indian Airlines' flight from Heathrow to Delhi. I preferred Indian Airlines; there was no quibbling over vegetarian meals.

The flight arrived in Delhi at 12:30 a.m. and I took the bus to the domestic airport for a flight to Bangalore. The airport was closed so I trundled my trolley around the adjoining streets looking for a tea stall, where I was joined by an Indian gentleman travelling alone. We found a tea stall selling chai and snacks where other stranded travellers had collected. The gentleman was a brain surgeon from England who was sharing his expertise, gratis, to help in local hospitals. I had no rupees as the banks in Delhi had been closed, but my new acquaintance kindly solved this problem by exchanging Rs.900 for £20. This enabled me to buy my ticket to Bangalore. In 1985 I did not have a credit card.

Back at the airport I checked in my suitcase, received my boarding ticket and proceeded to the plane. I was first up the gangway, unaware that the luggage was currently sitting on the tarmac waiting to be identified by its owners prior to boarding. With the plane ready for take-off I looked out of the window; here was my case sitting forlornly on the tarmac. I alerted the hostess, raced down the steps, boarded the bus back to departures, identified my case to staff and raced back to the plane.

It was a short flight to Bangalore, which is known as the Garden City due to its abundance of flowers and foliage. The airport bus trundled along the crowded streets as music blared and bright lights from cafes and restaurants lit up the jostling throngs. It was dark by the time I was dropped off in the middle of the city. Asking the driver for the Shilton Hotel, he pointed and said, 'Go that way.'

I picked up my case and was immediately surrounded by locals. 'Taxi? 'Auto rickshaw?' 'Coolie?' I chose the coolie, who had wrapped a dirty cloth around his head in anticipation. 'Shilton Hotel, please.' The man unwrapped his cloth and walked away. The rickshaw chap returned and without a word picked up my case. I repeated the address of the hotel and we set off. We went around in circles for half an hour, between the mass of people, cars, rickshaws and buses all vying for space amid much honking of horns. I was unaware that the driver did not know the hotel and was asking drivers and pedestrians for directions. Eventually a policeman helped us out. On arrival the irate driver demanded Rs.17. I handed the money over; he deserved it and it was only 70 pence.

My room was separate from the main building and very quiet, very comfortable, large and en-suite. Settling in I had a much-needed pot of tea with samosas on the terrace, where I met Elene from Greenland. We were constantly interrupted by waiters asking for a cigarette. I had made the mistake of giving a pack to one of them and now they all wanted one. Elene told me that she had come to India to see her guru, Sai Baba. I had not heard of him but, checking in, I had seen a

poster of a man with a crinkly Afro hairstyle wearing a burgundy robe: Sai Baba, who was highly revered in the area.
'Who is he?' I had inquired.

Elene told me that she was travelling to Puttaparti the next
day to see Sai Baba at his ashram. Before I could question her
further she'd spotted an Indian gentleman and his son, waving
for her attention. The waiter, now my friend, told me Elene
was sharing a taxi in the morning with the men who were also
Baba devotees. This sounded interesting. I asked them if I
might go along too and was welcomed. Cars are scarce and
sharing is cheaper.

We set off at the crack of dawn. We drove through villages,
past tea plantations, grape vineyards and coconut groves.
Smiling friendly people, beggars showing wide, toothless grins,
hands outstretched, reached for the open window. There were
boys with smooth skin, liquid-brown eyes and cheeky grins.
Five hours later after several chai stops and aching from
bumping along on broken springs, we arrived at the Abode of
Great Peace.

The taxi passed through the gates of the ashram and in to a
narrow road with low buildings. Beyond this, the ground
opened into an area of three-storey buildings set in rows a few
feet apart. This was the accommodation where we would have
space in a shared room for Rs.5.I asked for a room to myself
but was refused– all other rooms were occupied. Ours was
small with a concrete floor, a toilet, washbasin and a tiny
window with shutters but no glass. The wooden door had an
iron bar and padlock on the outside. Our travelling companions went to another building. We had one key between us.
For sleeping arrangements, Elene commandeered the wall

away from the open window and I the other, below the window. We decided we would take turns to have the key. We locked up, and went to explore.

The Indian ladies wore colourful saris or long, flowing skirts with tops concealing their shoulders and breasts. Most Westerners wore white. This was the accepted dress, and Elene was planning to visit the local dress shop that would make an outfit for her. She suggested I accompany her. I had left most of my clothes at the Shilton, and was currently dressed in loose, green pants and a multi-coloured blouse. They would have to do as my budget would not stretch to new clothes – especially those worn only once.

We set off for the shop outside the ashram. As newcomers, we were surrounded by coolies urging us to buy a mattress and, recalling the stone floor, this sounded like a good idea but I decided not to rush into it. Elene, on the other hand, seemed to understand the ashram and being a devotee wanted every-thing necessary, including a mattress. Only later did I discover that I could have borrowed a mattress free, gratis and for nothing, from the office. (I did not mention this to Elene as she had spent a fair amount of money at the shop.)She also bought a pillow, cushion and a scarf to cover her upper anatomy and was measured for a white sari that would be ready for collection in an hour. 'Nothing for me, thank you,' I said. Elene looked pointedly at my breasts unadorned by scarf or jacket. I conceded and bought a large white scarf.

Lunch was next on the agenda and we bought vouchers for Rs.2.50. Tea was a few paise extra. All meals were vegetarian, which suited me. Men and women ate in separate halls –long rooms with six or seven stone tables that stretched the length of the room separated by aisles. We presented our meal vouchers to the servers– all volunteers –who ladled curry, yoghurt and chapattis on to tin plates. Drinking water was available. Food was eaten by hand or, as a sop to Westerners, with a plastic spoon. Tea was served in the men's hall, which I thought odd, as segregation seemed to be an unwritten law of sleeping accommodation and shared spaces.

At 2:30 p.m. we joined the throng at the temple waiting to catch a glimpse of Sai Baba. Elene looked cool in her white outfit while I remained multi-coloured, a white scarf draped modestly over my shoulders hiding any sign of femininity.

A large, open, sandy area surrounded the temple. A low wall beyond contained more sand where men and ladies sat cross-legged but segregated. We sat in orderly rows, the Indian ladies in colourful saris blended in. I felt we were intruders, however, if that were so, there were hundreds of us from all over the European continent. I waited in suspenseful anticipation. Two elderly women brought a bag of numbered tokens and the first lady in each row took a number. As the numbers were called out a row of ladies arose and sat down in front of the temple beyond the wall. Eventually, it was our turn and we were seated in the last row away from the temple. Elene plumped her cushion and sat down. I had no cushion but, being well-padded, rested on the hard sand.

This procedure lasted a long time and my legs, not used to yoga-like positions, were cramped. By 4:30 p.m. I was very uncomfortable indeed. When Sai Baba appeared, a sudden hush descended. He walked part way up the rows of women, accepting letters but refusing presents. He repeated this for the men before entering his temple. I glanced at Elene who was crying with emotion. This was a big moment in her life and one for which she had waited a long time. I delved into my bag and offered her tissues.

I thought the ceremony was finished and I waited for the exodus to begin. But no one moved. I looked around and unfolding my legs from their painful position, wondered how much longer I could remain seated. Eventually I got up to stretch until, hearing music I re-joined my row as the *bhajan* started —the singing of sacred songs and chants. I hummed along while devotees sang and clapped. It finished at 6 p.m.

A lady was standing outside our room. Ruth, a recent arrival, had been allocated accommodation in number 11 – our room. I apologised, explaining there was no space. She insisted that the office had said there was no other place available. I accepted the inevitable, smiled reluctantly and introduced myself. I unlocked the door with the one and only key. She explained that she had not intended to visit the ashram as she had been here before. Travelling around India, she had spent two nights sleeping in a railway station, boarded the wrong train and now here she was. I thought this was strange but Ruth said it was Baba's way – he meant her to return. 'He exudes an aura,' she said, 'and if one is a devotee, it is absorbed.' I had absorbed nothing.

Our neighbour Bob was an Englishman and a devotee who had brought a party of Indian schoolchildren from England. I went in search of him to learn more. He related many stories surrounding Baba, tales of healing crippled children, of producing objects from thin air and of appearing to people when in need of help. Bob told me that this Baba was an incarnation of a previous Sai Baba who had died at Shirdi in 1918. When

I remained sceptical, Bob gave me a book entitled: *Sai Baba, Man of Miracles*, by Howard Murphet. I thanked him, threw it in my bag with no intention of reading it and returned to my room, now occupied by a Greenlander, an English lady and a Scot.

Elene related more stories of Baba. She produced a small bag containing ash and persuaded me to swallow some and smear a little on my brow. I wondered where it had come from. Evidently, Baba had produced it from the air and given it to his devotees for its healing powers. Enough! I went for a walk and, on the way, met a history teacher who mentioned that the well-constructed buildings were part of a university, secondary and primary school built by Sai's volunteer army of tradesmen.

That evening we three chatted. Ruth spoke of her mother's disapproval of her roaming India. She then asked my age. I was taken aback – travellers are ships that pass in the night and have an unwritten code of not asking personal questions. I told her I never divulged my age but had three lovely children. She considered this, said age did not matter and travelling was not just for the young. I had never felt so old.

We lay down to sleep on the stone floor beside our respective walls. Ruth on a blanket and Elene on her mattress fell asleep instantly. I swatted mosquitoes from where I lay on a torn bamboo mat, a relic from a previous devotee. Later, halfway through the night, Elene woke up screaming. I jumped up and switched on the light to see a very large cockroach on the move. We three looked at each other challengingly. Who was going to kill it? In Hong Kong my husband and sons had always done the slaughtering while I stood on a chair. Elene continued to scream, Ruth had crawled into a corner cuddling the wall. So be it, the dirty work was left to me. I picked up a shoe and slapped at the offending beastie. It was quick off the mark, scuttling all over the place with Elene jumping out of the way at each turn. Eventually, I cornered it and managed to deal the deathblow. The other two went back to sleep with sighs of relief but, turning off the light, my eye caught a movement high on the wall, where a small army of cockroaches clung. I said nothing but spent a sleepless night hitting out at imaginary – or real – cockroaches running over me.

As daylight crept through the shutters, exhausted I took stock and decided this was not my bowl of rice. I decided to leave for Bangalore. Elene and Ruth had risen at 4 a.m. to join a torch-light procession around the temple. I awaited their return, said goodbye and caught the bus back. Tired and weary after a long, bumpy ride, I reclaimed my suitcase, had a shower and was about to climb into bed when there was a knock at the door. A waiter. Was he bringing me a cup of tea? No, a wide smile and an endearing look in his wistful brown eyes and he procured his pack of cigarettes. Thank goodness no one had smoked at the ashram or I would have none left. Bed beckoned. I fell into a deep sleep.

The next day, gazing into the mirror, I barely recognised myself. Bags under my eyes, hair in disarray, a mosquito bite crimson-red on sun dappled cheeks. It was definitely time for some T.L.C. so I visited the Ashok Hotel for a hairdo. When travelling in India, I usually stayed at cheap hotels (although none so cheap as the ashram),but always sought out a luxury hotel where I could purchase postcards, stamps, maps and brochures and have a wash in an upmarket toilet. After my pampering session, I hired an auto-rickshaw that took me on a tour. On our route I noticed the Bangalore Golf Club, paid off the driver and entered. At reception I asked if there were reciprocal arrangements with the Hong Kong Golf Club of which I was a member. There wasn't, but the manager greeted me and kindly offered a set of clubs, a caddy, a partner and a round of golf. I accepted the partner, Prasad, but declined the golf as it was rather hot, and instead accepted Prasad's offer to sit and relax on the cool veranda. Several members offered to buy drinks and I spent a very pleasant evening in the company of friendly, hospitable people. Later, Prasad drove me around town and into the countryside where he pointed out another Sai Baba ashram. It transpired that it had not been necessary to go on an uncomfortable five-hour cross-country ride to Puttaparti.

Our current mode of transport was a motor-bike and my white trousers were not exactly a sensible mode of dress. Prasad was from Bangalore, working in technology in the 'Silicon Valley' of India. It was a busy city with a teeming population, abundant tropical flora and well laid out gardens. Prasad zoomed in and out of traffic with ease and daring. My hair unravelled behind me in the breeze and my white trousers had taken on a distinct grey hue by the time we reached the Shilton. I climbed painfully and unsteadily from the bike. I need not have bothered visiting the hairdresser! I thanked him and offered tea. This was declined, as he had to go to work.

The following day, I packed my rucksack and flew to Mysore in Karnataka state where my Dharamsala friend's brother, Llawang, was studying in college. The rickshaw driver deposited me at a hotel. That night after dinner I wandered the streets where bullock carts, pony traps, auto rickshaws and cows vied for space. The cow is sacred and if one stopped at the roadside to munch the foliage, rather than shoo it away a traffic jam would form. Displayed on stalls and in shops were shoes, saris, sacks of millet, coconuts and coffee beans.

Having previously contacted Llawang by phone, we met in Brindavan Gardens where he introduced me to his charming sisters, Dolma and Cholden, who attended secondary school. It was hard for the Tibetans: they had to learn Hindi, the national language; Kanada, the local dialect and were taught mostly in English. The girls' father had died in Dharamsala. Their mother lived in a refugee centre in the south where she had a smallholding, a plot of land given by the Indian government to each Tibetan family who had settled there to help them be self-sufficient.

These lovely gardens had well laid out paths, a variety of tropical colourful flowers and a coconut grove. At night, illuminated fountains were a spectacular sight. After a meal and a fond farewell, I returned to the hotel to book a trip by coach to Ooty Hill Station. Much of the scenery on the way reminded me of Scotland. Monkeys and elephants inhabited the nearby jungle.

The next day I left for Bangalore where I reclaimed my case from the Shilton. While I was taking a shower there was a knock on the door. Dripping wet, I wrapped a towel around me and opened a crack. It was Raju the waiter, again asking for cigarettes. I thrust a pack through. I was making a lot of waiters in the south very happy or very rich. The cigarettes, I suspected, were probably being sold on, one at a time.

The following day I flew to Delhi and subsequently to Heathrow. There is a sequel to the ashram story; unknown to me at the time, I was to return. As the lady who had got on the wrong train mentioned, if Sai Baba wants you back, back you will go.

Back in London I arranged to visit my son Gordon and daughter-in law Angela. I bought a bunch of daffodils, dithered over buying wine and caught the underground to Clapham. I was wearing a circular-shaped, gold-coloured pendant watch encrusted with small, glass, coloured beads. As I walked the watch bounced on my chest. The bright sun glancing off the colourful beads must have given the appearance of emeralds, sapphires, diamonds and rubies.

Suddenly two coffee-coloured hands grabbed my shoulder and spun me around. I came face to face with my attacker who lunged for my watch. He snatched at the chain but it did not break. I defended myself with the daffodils, regretting I had not bought the wine, as a bottle would have made a nice crack on his head. At the same time I kicked him and he backed off. We stood regarding each other until a tinkle heralded the watch falling to the ground. I stooped to pick it up and he resumed his attack. But I was ready for him and he backed off into the road. Suddenly, a small boy of about twelve appeared from nowhere. He was the same colour as my mugger and I asked him what I should do. 'Go home,' he said. My assailant then ran off. The boy disappeared as suddenly and mysteriously as he had appeared.

Stumbling to my son's door I handed over three battered daffodils and sank down feeling rather shaken. After I'd explained what had happened, Gordon phoned the police. A policeman and woman arrived exclaiming, 'Congratulations.' They were impressed that I still possessed my watch. The police bundled me into their car and we drove around the area but my mugger had long since disappeared. We drove on to the police station where I was shown a file of mug shots from which to identify him – in vain. 'Well' I said, 'I'm going back to a civilised city tomorrow. Glasgow.' There was a great deal of loud laughter and I left the station puzzling over what was so funny. I supposed the Metropolitan Police had their little jokes.

When I arrived home and unpacked, I found the book about Sai Baba and sat down to read. I came across a paragraph that mentioned how he often helped devotees who were in trouble, and that he could transport himself to any location. I thought of the boy who had appeared out of nowhere when I was attacked. I became a devotee, returning to the ashram some years later. The scenery had changed, but not only that, I saw the ashram with different eyes, although not rose-coloured.

Returning to the ashram, I managed to get floor space with three Greek ladies. It was Sai Baba's birthday and the place was heaving with followers. The ashram had grown; it was now the length of two football fields. My room, which was marginally larger than my previous one, was in a new building called the Roundhouse. There were now two canteens serving a choice of Western and Indian food. I had daal, rice, vegetables and sauce. Western fare was macaroni with tomato sauce and mild spicy potato, cauliflower and tea, milk, ices and fresh coconut. There was no shortage of food and I never heard of anyone being ill.

The ceremony was just as before. I was sitting in the back row, distanced from Baba as he walked around. He looked up at me. Tears filled my eyes and for a moment I felt a presence that I could not explain. It was an experience that I will never forget.

At 6:30 p.m. there was dancing in one of the fields. Large statues of Christ, Buddha and Shiva (an Indian God), were raised. Baba preached love and embraced all religions. He encouraged business people to sell up and go forth to help the disadvantaged.

Lights out was at 9:30 p.m. with an early rising at 4:30 a.m. to attend the temple for Darshan. The organisation was amazing. We sat in rows as before, hundreds of men and women sitting cross-legged and silent in segregated areas. Students from Baba's schools were included. After his appearance and his usual walk around, he chose a few devotees to join him in the temple, where he listened to their problems and dispensed advice. We dispersed at 7:40 a.m.

My mind was not totally consumed with the idea of entering the temple. I was engrossed with mundane matters like trying to remember when the restaurant and shops were open. I bought photographs of Baba, mineral water and a toilet roll. I met with a Danish lady, Rodriguez, who had recently finished a book on Baba. She would not return to Denmark as she found life there empty, bare and lonely. But staying on was discouraged and she was unhappy at the thought of leaving.

On my previous visit I had endured sleepless nights. Now Ria, one of the Greek ladies, gave me a mattress and sleeping became more manageable. There were mosquito nets over the windows and door but the incessant humming of the few insects that managed to sneak through was disturbing. But there were no cockroaches.

I spoke to Australians, Mexicans, Indonesians, Europeans, Japanese and Americans– a right United Nations. The majority were Indian and I did not hear a British voice; perhaps I was carrying the candle for the U.K. Most come in groups from Sai organisations, his influence having spread far and wide. Instead of saying 'hello', the words 'Sai Ram' were used as a greeting and to mean 'excuse me'. All very peaceful. It was one of the few places where there was no sexual aggression– remarkable considering the number of men and women living there. Facilities included a post office and telephone system. An airline office was due soon. Sai had also built a hospital that I wanted to see but special permission was required. I became the Scottish delegation for overseas' aid– and got in. Treatment was free for everyone. There was a blood bank, surgery and a urology unit– all funded by donations.

Although the hospital was already in use it would be another year before completion. Built in the shape of an 'OM'– that is Shanti, or universal peace – it was so large that when Baba visited he drove a buggy-type vehicle to get around.

It was time for me to move on and I arranged to leave by bus the next day. I bought chapattis and cheese, packed my rucksack, folded the mattress and wrote a note to Ria. Passing the courtyard on my way out an organiser gestured for me to join in. I shrugged my shoulders, indicating the want of a large scarf, but she nodded for me to join anyway. So there was I once more, scrunched up, yoga position, sitting in tight formation despite my vow of never again. Sai Baba wins.

The bus journey was the usual hair-raising ride. It was scary to see oxen carts careering down the middle of the road heading straight for the bus. Our experienced driver skilfully used the dirt shoulders to avoid a collision. Bicycles, rickshaws, taxis, people and cows claimed the centre. Fortunately, we reached Bangalore in one piece.

The End

Russia via China & Mongolia

❧

CHINA

In 1983 I decided to visit Russia by the Trans-Mongolian Railway via China and Mongolia. My journey began with an early morning departure by steamboat from the capitalist colony of Hong Kong into the heart of communist China.

My first problem was to find a travel agent who could handle my many and varied bookings, but after asking several I found they were not interested in a lone traveller. I eventually found Travel Advisors and Time Travel who were extremely helpful. That accomplished, I required visas, one each for China, Mongolia and Russia. This was to be a tricky operation as I could only get the latter two in Peking and they had to be issued on the same day. And the embassies opened at different times and only briefly. Nothing in China is consistent, and office hours can change overnight.

Having succeeded in getting my China visa in Hong Kong, I packed a suitcase and backpack. The pier at the docks opened to passengers at 12:40 p.m. We passed through the Hong Kong terminal and immigration. First, we boarded a small ferry that carried us to the Shanghai Steam boat anchored off Stonecutters Island. This was not an easy transfer as our ferry had very narrow, steep steps to a lighter at the foot of the gangway, also with steep and narrow steps. I was one of the first on board and amused myself watching from the deck as passengers struggled to ascend with television sets, radios, folding beds – everything and the kitchen sink most of which dangled from the ends of bamboo poles. These goods were destined for families in China. At that time China had a one-child policy but Russia was offering financial help to encourage couples to have children.

A stewardess escorted me to first-class cabin A; en-suite, with a curtained deck window, bunk, bedside light, small wardrobe, dining table and drawers, carpeted floor and air conditioning. There was a large flask of hot water, a tin of jasmine tea and a large Chinese-style cup. Double doors led into the corridor, effectively shutting out noise. It was comfortable.

The boat glided silently out of the harbour at 4:45p.m. by which time I had explored the interior. There was a bar, lounge, cafeteria and cinema but no films. There were dormitory style metal bunks, two-tiers high, in lines of eight with a large lounge in the centre. There was one toilet for men and one for women. Meal times were staggered according to cabin class. Dinner was served from 6 p.m. and consisted of dumplings, rice, steamed chicken, fish soup and vegetables. I enjoyed the meals and this leisurely way of entering China through the South China Sea, passing sampans, fishing junks, oil tankers, launches and yachts.

At 9 a.m. the next day, we entered the muddy waters of the Huangpu river, where Chinese navy boats nestled at their docks and we were warned not to take photographs. The buildings were solid with not a high-rise in sight. Immigration officials came aboard and after form-filling and passport inspection, the passengers were allowed to disembark.

My hotel, the Pujiang near Shanghai Mansions, was within walking distance beside the river. There were five beds in the room at six yuan each. They had very thin, hard, heavy mattresses covered in clean white cotton covers. The room was large with a wooden floor, two wooden frame windows, an old dressing table and a telephone. The bathroom was tiled, had high ceilings, hot water and a bath. The hotel had two dining rooms.

I explored the city, discovered the Yu Yuan Gardens and sat sipping tea in the Wing Xing Ting teahouse where I observed the ritual of the tea ceremony. It was an old wooden pavilion; the interior was cool and contained typically hard, wooden Chinese-style chairs and a high altar table with lovely carving. I walked over the wooden zigzag bridge designed to ward off evil spirits, watched carp in the pool, passed weeping willow trees, grottos, bamboo and root carvings of dragons and figures. I walked back to the hotel along a wide street crowded with pedestrians. There were so many bicycles on the road that I could hear the wheels humming from a distance. Cars resembled old black Vauxhalls and there were army trucks and trolley buses. The intersections were wide; traffic was controlled by a man sitting in a round tower. There were no traffic lights, but white lines for pedestrians to cross the road at their peril.

The next morning after breakfast I was asked to leave the hotel. I refused. Communication was difficult. Eventually, another guest told me that I had to pay for the bed each morning to secure it for that night, as it was not permitted to pay in advance for the week. That settled, I wandered down to the Bund – the garden by the riverside. Here, girls, boys and adults crowded around me to practice their English. At night, I went to the Peace Hotel where there was a fantastic band that played music from the 1940s and 50s. The band members were quite old but their music was obviously remembered fondly from the decadent days of colonialism. The room was packed with foreigners, no locals allowed. There were only three women so we danced the night away with a succession of male partners.

I had enjoyed Shanghai and its friendly people but it was now time to move on. I bought a train ticket to Peking. It was an overnight journey and there were three types of sleeping arrangement: soft sleeper, hard sleeper and hard seat. Foreigners were expected to travel soft sleeper, however, I wanted to be with the locals so opted for hard sleeper. My compartment had six bunks with an open corridor – no privacy here. A flask of hot water was provided and as I had brought Chinese tea, I could help myself at any hour. The friendly Chinese shared their food, and staff walked past selling eggs and chicken.

There were six bunks, four of which were folded down during the day. Four bunks were occupied by Chinese men and the fifth by a European lady. We women were in the top bunks and did not sleep very well as it was so cramped with barely enough space between bunk and ceiling. The Chinese on the bottom bunks had paid half price. There was only a thin wall between compartments. One of the men, Chen Hong, who had been to Russia, taught me a few Russian words. He was, however, wary of speaking English - security police were everywhere - and so we conversed in French –mine limited – in hushed voices. As a thank you I gave him my small radio (little realising that trouble awaited this gesture). At night when I was sleeping he slipped a small, plastic weather windmill under my pillow. This would have been for his children and I was mortified when he refused to take it back. The Chinese return a present with a present – a fact I had forgotten. They are a generous race.

Our train passed through Suzhou, Wuxi and Nanjing where millions of trees were planted 30 years ago. The land was flat with wheat crops, vegetables and rice paddies. Lunch was served in the dining room but people in the compartment shared their food. We had mandarin oranges, sweets, cheese, chocolate and tea whilst sitting on our bunks chatting. We were due to arrive in Peking at 10 a.m. and I needed to find a hotel. I also needed to visit the Mongolian and Russian embassies for visas. Friday found me saying goodbye to Chen Hong and the others as the train pulled into the station.

Finding a room in a hotel was not easy – none wanted foreigners. I caught a taxi to the Quanghua Hotel and was refused entry. I returned to the station and caught a bus to the Bei Wei Hotel: no rooms. I began to think this was a conspiracy by the Chinese International Tourist Service (C.I.T.S.). My next attempt was the Sportsman Inn, without success. I was feeling frustrated at not being permitted to stay in a hotel. Where was I going to spend the night? I could only surmise that these refusals were due to the authorities wanting to know where foreigners were at all times. At the C.I.T.S offices I was told to return to the Sportsman Inn where I managed to book in this time. Now, the authorities knew exactly where I was, however the Sportsman Hotel was convenient as it was beside the Temple of Heavenly Peace and a short bus ride to the Forbidden Palace, Tiananmen Square and the Summer Palace.

All this running around was tiring but, because time was short, I now had to book my tickets for the Trans-Mongolian train. I could not board the train without Mongolian and Russian visas, which I was unable to obtain until several days later as the embassies were shut. Moreover, I was not permitted to pay for the ticket until I had the visas. I returned to the hotel at 7 p.m. to be allocated a room by reception. By this time I was very tired and looking forward to a nice hot shower, but there was no hot water so I had a cold one, washed my hair and fell into bed exhausted. What a hassle it is travelling in China. Not enjoyable, but interesting. The next day I was keen to hear English voices and so phoned the British Embassy to gain entry to the only pub in China, the Bell. I was made very welcome at the bar and chatted to several Englishmen.

To fill in time prior to obtaining my visas I roamed Peking, walking and using buses. I passed through Tiananmen Square and the Forbidden City, which is so enormous with its huge courtyards that I did not manage to see it all. This had been the emperor's palace and covered approximately 180 acres. I also wanted to see the Great Wall but a tour organised by C.I.T.S. cost 50 yuan, whereas I could buy a ticket for 7 yuan at a local ticket office across the road. This was not a simple matter as the first answer to my enquiry was, 'No, not permitted.' Foreigners were not welcome in China, that was obvious, but I was becoming accustomed to this negativity and persisted, refusing to budge from the window until I was sold a ticket.

I stopped at the Friendship store to buy bread and cheese for a picnic. The shop was run by the authorities and was where foreigners could buy Western food from a dairy and a supermarket. It reminded me of my first stay in Hong Kong in 1959, when the only place to buy European food was the Dairy Farm shop. I also bought tea and some luxuries in preparation for my Trans-Mongolian trip.

I caught the bus at 7:50 a.m. the next day. It crawled through the already busy city and out into the countryside. We were stopped at the guarded entrance to the Wall and allowed two hours for sight-seeing. Built in 221AD by the Chinese emperor Qin Shi Huang to protect China from invasion by the Mongol hordes, it was now mostly ruins, although some parts had been re-built. I strolled along until I could go no further. It was an amazing sight.

We drove on to the tombs where the Ming Emperors (1368-1644) were buried. Stone statues of animals, lions, camels and figures guarded the entrance. I entered a courtyard, walked through a pagoda and down some stairs to the tombs. There was not much to see: a stone bench, a few red boxes and stone slabs and no guide to relate the history. The bus returned to the city and I went to bed early in preparation for my visit on Monday to the embassies to procure my visas. Since the Trans-Mongolian train ran only on a Wednesday, it was imperative that I should get to the embassies that day. And besides, the embassies were only open for a short time for visa applications, and not every day.

I visited the C.I.T.S. office for information on embassy times and just managed to squeeze into the Russian embassy before the doors closed. I handed over my passport, a photograph and US$4. I was told to return the next day to collect my visa. Then on to the Mongolian embassy to join the queue there. I was nervously biting my nails as the queue moved so slowly and the office was only open for an hour. Fortunately, when the doors shut leaving many outside, I was in, paying US$2. for my visa.

With my two visas I returned to C.I.T.S. on Tuesday and paid for the train ticket. Relief. I was going to make it.

At 7:30 a.m. the following day I boarded the Trans-Mongolian train from Peking railway station passing through the International Departure lounge. As before, there were different classes of sleeper: deluxe, first-class, soft and hard. I chose hard which was actually very comfortable. There were four berths and I shared with two other ladies, one German and one English. A bedroll was provided and there was storage space within the bunks for luggage. A flask was available for hot water filled from a machine at the end of each carriage. There was a bed light, a main light, a fan, heating, blinds, a table and a speaker for announcements.

The long train left on time chugging slowly out of the station, passing the Great Wall, through several tunnels prior to picking up speed. The picture window gave a view of flat land with crops in the foreground and hills beyond changing to desert, flat and colourless. A few sheep and horses grazed by the verge. As we passed various stations, railway officials stood to attention along the platform until we were out of sight. As we approached the Mongolian border and stopped at the last border town of Datong, passengers removed the film from their cameras in case the officials who came on board opened and exposed them. We stayed there for three hours while passports were examined and the declaration forms, which we had filled in on the Shanghai-Peking train, were scrutinised by officials. I had not known that these forms were passed on to customs'. I had declared the little radio that I had since given to Chen Hong. Now I was asked to produce it for inspection. Unable to do so, I was invited into the customs' building where I explained that I had broken it and it now lay in a dustbin in Peking. I was fined 10 yuan. Having been kept waiting for some time I was now thirsty, so when I espied officers drinking tea and smoking in a rest room I joined them.

When they discovered I was a teacher of English, I spent the next two hours giving English lessons to six officers, after which a tape recorder was produced for me to read and record customs forms. A good Scots accent was obviously well understood.

MONGOLIA

Time to go and I was escorted to the train. As we left, the customs men and women lined up on the platform. Their khaki uniforms were immaculate; their crimson high-boned cheeks shone in the station lights. We crossed into Jiding in Outer Mongolia. I was very tired; I had drunk endless cups of Chinese tea and smoked a lot whilst enjoying the friendly hospitality. I was unable to sleep, disturbed by the noisy changes from gauge to gauge during which we had to exit the train while the carriages were jacked up. We finally rolled out at 1.30 a.m. Breakfast, Mongolian style, was stuffed pancakes with jam, bread and tea for US$1; butter was extra.

The land was desolate with mountains as a backdrop. Small quaint houses dotted the landscape. Camels and cows grazed alongside. The train stopped for half an hour at Ulan Bator, enabling us to stretch our legs. The Mongolians had high, coloured cheeks with broad faces of a Slavic nature. Some had European features with fair skin and hair. A few wore western-style clothing; others long brown tunics with long sleeves and trousers tucked into boots. Some houses were small and wooden, but there were also high-rises of about ten storeys. On the horizon, yurts were scattered across the grasslands. When the train pulled away from the station at 3 p.m. the dining car opened for lunch of tomatoes, rice and omelette. It was now very cold as the landscape opened to hills and trees topped with snow, rivers, and rich brown and black tilled fields.

We stopped at the last station in Mongolia where our passports were checked. It was 6 p.m. on my watch but time was confusing – was it Chinese or Mongolian time? Later, we stopped at the Russian border for another check. Customs officers came aboard looking for magazines and books of some description, although we never found out what. Perhaps pornography or books banned in Russia? At 10 p.m. we retrieved our passports but when the train passed into Russia, surrendered them again. The customs check was very strict. We were ordered into the corridor by soldiers. There were no hiding places but bunks were lifted, rifles poked along the high shelf, toilets were closed and the samovar shut off. I attempted to leave the train but was pushed roughly back in line. When I looked out of the window there were soldiers with rifles lining the platform. Who, in their right mind, would want to smuggle themselves into Russia, I wondered? Apparently, the Chinese ambassador was in the next carriage, which may have accounted for such an officious welcome. When all carriages had been thoroughly checked we were allowed off the train to change currency at a bank on the platform: dollars into roubles, with ten dollars equal to seven roubles. Only roubles could be used in the dining car and the bank would not accept traveller's cheques. Russia wanted only American currency. The train left at 1:30 a.m.

RUSSIA

After a delicious breakfast of fried eggs, a bottle of milk, cocoa, bread, butter and cheese, the train approached Irkutsk, my destination. This interesting trip had taken two and a half days but had been tiring, caught out by customs', harassed by soldiers. Thankful to be leaving I packed my case, hoisted my backpack and waved goodbye to my fellow passengers who were continuing to Poland.

In Russia, tourists are met by an official from INTourist, the Russian travel agency affiliated to government. I wandered round the station for some time but when no one seemed interested in me I entered an office and announced my presence.

I spoke to the manager who contacted INTourist. Within ten minutes a bus appeared with driver and an English-speaking official, Sergei, who apologised for not being at the station to greet me. We drove to Hotel INTourist, a modern white building where I was shown a room with bed, table, couch and television that did not work. As in all Russian hotels there was a woman on each floor called a key lady. She sits at a desk outside the lift, helps guests and monitors their coming and going. There was a samovar on each floor so constant hot water for tea was available.

After accepting the room, I checked-in, handed over my passport, deposited my luggage, showered, changed and inquired at the INTourist desk about the night life. 'Nyet.' There was none. I walked to a park beside the Angura river, where a little girl walking with her father presented me with a bunch of flowers. Delighted, I thanked her in my best Russian. In return her father thanked me in English– I don't know why. How did he know I was British? Strolling on, I got into conversation with two men, Vladimir and Mark, who asked if I had any new jeans for sale. After a chat, I was invited to dinner at the local nightspot, the Hotel Siberia, where we danced the night away with vodka and Champagne. So much for INTourist stopping foreigners exploring. The tables were full, Champagne corks popped non-stop, a band played decadent Western music both old and new. The women were well-dressed, but reminded me of British fashion twenty years before. Many had harshly dyed blonde or red hair, bee-hive style. Afterwards, we sat by the river until midnight. When the evening was over, I was escorted to my hotel but when I invited my companions to join me for a drink, they were forbidden. Russians were barred.

Nursing a monumental hangover the next day, I approached INTourist to enquire about local buses to Lake Baikal. This was met with a firm, 'Nyet.' No local buses went to Baikal. I knew, however, that where people worked, there were buses.

I walked into town and accosted strangers uttering, 'Baikal'. The locals were very helpful and in broken English conveyed they were sorry that they could not communicate more effectively. They were mainly Czechs and spoke German, of which I had no knowledge. I was passed on from person to person until I reached the stop. The local houses were an odd combination, some were of solid stone, and others were new, brick apartment houses sporting television aerials and chimneys.

Tucked at the back were little wooden houses with painted shutters. Children played, old men and women sat on benches chatting and eating ice cream. When I reached the bus stop I enlisted the aid of a lady who put me on the correct bus. It was crowded. I was gently chivvied along by the passengers, not allowed to sit down until I reached an 'honesty' box in the middle of the bus (I found out the name later). There was no conductor. I put my fare in, took a ticket and finally I could sit.

The people and the language so fascinated me that I missed the stop. Before I realised it, the bus was on the return journey so I got off at the next stop and approached a young man standing nearby. I managed to convey that I wanted Lake Baikal. He kindly escorted me to the correct bus, paid my fare, and took me to the pier at Paketa where I bought a round-trip ticket for the hovercraft for roubles 2.60, which was very cheap. I went downstairs on the craft and sat on a comfortable padded bench. Beer, sandwiches, juice and cigarettes were on sale. As the craft sped across the lake the picture windows provided a view of trees lining the shores, the background dominated by snow-capped mountains. We alighted at an island where I took photographs. This created much interest from other passengers, who wished to be included in my snaps, although they would never see them. When I tried to re-board the ferry, I had a moment of panic when I was not allowed on. Then one of the crew took me to the ticket counter where I had to buy another ticket– so much for a return!

When I boarded, a drunken Russian was sitting on the bench. He gradually slid closer and closer muttering in his vodka-smelling breath. Fortunately, Vera the stewardess, noticed my distress and came to my rescue. We went out on deck where she shared her cigarettes. Some soldiers, who were smoking, joined us and bought us beer and cigarettes. It was rather windy and I was given a uniform jacket and cap, thus cementing Russian-Scottish relations. They were very nice, friendly and amusing, and although we could not speak each other's languages we managed to communicate amid a great deal of laughter.

When we landed back at Paketa, Vera – now off-duty – and the soldiers accompanied me on the bus to Irkutsk and paid my fare. This was so generous as salaries were not high. We were a merry band, the soldiers singing and the passengers indulging them. Vera and I alighted, waved goodbye to our companions and sat by the banks of the Angura drinking and smoking. Goods were scarce and I was sorry I had nothing with which to repay her kindness. I rummaged in my rucksack and found a lipstick, small return that it was. When we parted, I took her address and promised to write. I do not think Vera ever received my letters; Russia did not encourage relations with foreigners and the population was wary of authority.

I returned to the hotel, collected my passport and informed INTourist I would leave for Moscow in the morning. Breakfast consisted of peas, apple juice, tea with sugar, sour cake and sour cream. Sergei, the INTourist officer came to fetch me, picked up my suitcase and knapsack and led me to the coach. We were the only two passengers. As the bus drove off, I waved goodbye to Irkutsk.

Sergei settled down to read. When I noticed he was reading an English book I delved into my rucksack and produced a couple of books about Robert Burns, our Scottish bard of the 1700s (1759 -1796).He was delighted with the gift and told me that he had studied Burns in school. Well, why not?

At the airport I boarded an Aeroflot plane to Moscow. We took off as Western music played. The first stop was Omsk. I was unaware that an INTourist member was waiting to escort foreigners to a security transit lounge. Instead, I followed the other passengers through the main airport building and out, to explore the town. It occurred to me, rather late, that I did not know the time of departure and so I returned to the airport. It took me some time to make myself understood but when I was, my arm was seized by a hostess and we rushed to where the plane sat forlornly in a far corner of the runway. It had been there for some time waiting for the missing passenger. I climbed the gangway. The crew, including the captain stood in a line to greet me. I apologised profusely but was informed that it was their fault. INTourist should have looked after me. (I doubted the plane would have waited for a Russian passenger and felt quite guilty).The passengers said nothing but as I walked to my seat, 'tsk, tsk, tsk' was loud and clear. I think the problem was that, as in India, a lone woman traveller was not the norm.

When the plane landed in Moscow I received V.I.P.treatment. Nobody moved until a large man in a great-coat boarded, took charge and escorted me off to an INTourist waiting room. An official then whisked me and my baggage into a private car to the city. The airport is about 40 miles from Moscow and I settled back in comfort to watch the passing scenery. It was beautiful. Tall trees lined the broad road. We passed people walking in the forest and bathing in the river.

The driver stopped at the Hotel Nacionale, a multi-storey building for foreigners and Russian tourists, overlooking the Kremlin. Unlike in Irkutsk the staff were very off-hand and I guessed this was usual in a big city. My room had floorboards, pink walls, a table, comfortable bed, a television that did not work, a radio and en-suite facilities. After a shower I set out to explore Moscow. There was a beautiful building with a steeple and a star on the rooftop. Inside, great chandeliers hung the length of the hall and old-style lamps were built into niches, lighting the way and reflecting off the marble floor. I was disappointed to find it had been converted into flats and a shopping mall. I wondered what it had been in the days of the Tsars.

The women were neatly dressed, but in a fashion which reminded me of Britain about ten years before. I was quite hungry by now and returned to the hotel for a meal. On arrival, I had been given an identification card to present at meal times. When I ordered, the staff refused to serve me. However, the key lady on my floor, learning of my predicament, brought chicken noodle soup with cucumber salad and bread that was only just edible. Breakfast in the dining room consisted of fried eggs, sour milk, bread, cheese, jam and tea. Meals were difficult. I had to wait to be seated, wait to order and wait for food to be served. It was not enjoyable: eating for the sake of eating. It was simpler to eat in the room or in a restaurant. It was interesting to note that the Russians used an abacus, the Chinese method of counting.

Moscow was so large that I would be unable to walk its length and breadth. Instead I had booked a tour of the city for £3 to be paid in foreign currency. The roads were about three times the normal size of British roads with buildings occupying a whole block. We passed St. Basil's Cathedral with its colourful, roof-top domes. At the Kremlin guards like toy soldiers practised their unique high-stepping march. At Lenin's coffin the soldiers changed every hour at three minutes to the hour. There was a very long queue to view the embalmed body of Lenin (Vladimir Ilyich Ulyanov, the godfather of the 1917 Bolshevik revolution). I joined it but it moved so slowly that I finally gave up, leaving the patriotic citizens in reverential silence.

The next day after breakfast I set off to travel the Moscow underground in search of Ivan the Terrible and the Tsar's hunting grounds and palace at Kolstinaya. I had difficulty locating the Metro but after asking a succession of people, finally did so. I descended the escalator to the sight of beautiful wood panelling and lighting, unlike any other metro I had ever seen. The stations were spotless, beautifully designed with marble tiles and friezes. I found my train by asking directions. Everyone was so friendly and 'though communication was limited by pointing to the map I was understood. Having got on the right train I now had to alight at the right station. I elicited this information by showing my neighbour a postcard of the palace and a nudge from him sent me on my way. I produced my card once more and was directed to the palace, now a museum. It was closed but there was a nice park nearby and I sat on the grass for a picnic before returning to the hotel. Police and soldiers were numerous on the streets. The police, in blue uniform, carried sticks or batons and stood at all crossroads, where they blew a whistle if one crossed against the lights.

The following day I wanted to take a ferry to Gorky Park but when I asked INTourist for directions the answer was, 'Nyet.' I was becoming used to this so, as before, I walked, asking locals who pointed me in the direction of the river Moskva. The trip was very pleasant. I had a picnic there prior to returning to the hotel. In the evening I went to the theatre and enjoyed an exciting mix of Cossack dancing, ballet, disco dancing and mime, very entertaining and colourful.

At breakfast I happened to share a table with an English woman. Once allocated a table we had to sit there for all meals. We compared notes and both found Moscow difficult for a tourist – very formal.

Because I like exercise, one morning I decided to use the hotel stairs. I walked through the swing doors beside my room and descended. I expected to reach reception but the stairs lead me to the basement where my heels click-clacked on the stone floor, loud and clear. This obviously alerted security as I heard a door open behind me. I turned to see a very large man in a very large greatcoat approaching. Without a word he grasped me firmly by the arm. I was propelled up some stairs to reception and deposited unceremoniously in a chair in the hall. I was beginning to look forward to men in very large greatcoats as they saved me a great deal of hassle. That afternoon when I returned in the lift the key lady followed me to see me safely ensconced in my room. KGB in the hotel? Maybe. He had certainly looked imposing, not to be argued with. I tried the swing doors again to find them firmly locked. It was time to leave for Leningrad. I collected my passport from reception and packed my case ready for the morning.

Breakfast consisted of meat, peas, apple juice, tea with sugar, no milk, a sour cake and cream. Vegetarian food was a problem: I do not think the word exists in the Russian vocabulary! Mostly, I bought bread and cheese to supplement my diet and I still had snacks from China. There was always nice soup on the menu. Food was scarce in the shops so for the locals queues were long and frustrating and they often found, on reaching the counter, that there was nothing left.

That evening an INTourist member took me to the railway station in a private car– probably to make sure I left. I boarded the Red Arrow night train for Leningrad in a small but comfortable single berth compartment, with two bed lights, an overhead light, mirror, coat hangers and a hand towel. The mattress was thin and encased in a white sheet. There was no dining room, but hot water was available for tea. The scenery was picturesque – miles of forest and wooden, doll-like houses.

On arrival at 8.30 a.m., I went to the INTourist office. I was taken in a taxi to the Hotel Astoria where British businessmen and foreign tourists stay. Built in 1902, it was earmarked by Hitler for a celebratory banquet after the fall of Leningrad. According to Hitler's plan of operations, Field Marshal Ritter von Leeb was expected to capture Leningrad within a month. The siege of Leningrad, also known as the Leningrad Blockade, began in September 1941 and lasted 900 days, during which time hundreds of thousands of citizens died of starvation, cold and disease.

The hotel was amazing: spacious, with marble floors and lovely carpets. Beautiful chandeliers adorned the ceilings. There were three dining rooms and a snack bar for breakfast, after which two bars opened at different times. A broad marble staircase, carpeted in red, led to the bedrooms. Mine was very comfortably furnished. There was a small chandelier, red carpet, four blue chairs, and apricot and white walls. Very peaceful. It overlooked St Isaac's church. The key lady was in position, but the atmosphere was more relaxed than Moscow and more enjoyable. The hotel was beautiful and old-fashioned. There were dances in the afternoon and evenings with a band playing old-time music.

Breakfast consisted of pancakes, salad, eggs, sour cream, cheese, butter, teas or coffee. At the dining table were two

British businessmen, John and Richard, who talked about the jetfoil sail to the Garden of Fountains at Petradvorets. The fountains cascade down the garden, separated by walls, adorned with golden statues of either men or animals. I visited the Hermitage, famous for its galleries of paintings. A ferry trip on the Neva ended my exploration for the day and I returned to the hotel exhausted. It was fun and interesting, but tiring communicating in simple English and sparse Russian. After a dinner of meatless borsch and an omelette, I met some Russians staying at the hotel. We sipped Champagne and danced the night away to disco music from the jukebox. I was thoroughly enjoying Leningrad. When the band finished we went for a walk to observe the 'White Nights'. These occur in May-June when it is never dark and the evenings merge into dawn. They last for only three weeks so I was very lucky to have been there at the right time.

In the morning I took a city tour and learned that Leningrad was originally named St. Petersburg (founded in 1703 by Peter the Great), became Petrograd and, in 1924 in honour of Lenin, Leningrad. (In 1991, a turning point in Soviet history, it reverted to St Petersburg.) We passed monuments beside which newly-weds, the brides dressed in traditional white, had their photographs taken. Big solid buildings of former glory now partitioned off into flats provided accommodation for many families. So much to see and do. I met so many friendly people who were eager to hear of an outside world of which they seemed to know very little. There were many Finns. Apparently they would hire a bus in Finland and come to Leningrad for a booze-up on cheap liquor, staying for three nights without a visa. Returning home, they would load their hired buses with vodka and Champagne.

My visa had run out. At 11 a.m. when it was time to leave, an INTourist car arrived to take me to the railway station to exit into Finland. INTourist was saving me the trouble of getting a taxi and haggling over a fare. On the train I met many nationalities and we swapped stories while splitting a bottle of Champagne. We stopped at the Russian border where customs officials searched my luggage with a fine toothcomb, collected our passports and searched the train for smugglers. Moving on, we stopped at the Finnish border, retrieved our passports and were allowed off the train to change money: U.S. $1 to 5.5 Finnish marks. It was an uneventful journey into Helsinki where a trip to the tourist office elicited a voucher for one night, with breakfast in the Hotel Academia for 65 marks. This hotel was occupied by students during the academic year and tourists in the summer.

Breakfast the next morning consisted of a smorgasbord of cold meat, cheese, brown bread and butter with marmalade and cereal. I had booked a two-berth cabin on the ferry to Stockholm for 95 marks (my route would be the cheapest way back to Britain). To pass the time until sailing, I wandered around the shops and, although the clothes were lovely, they were too expensive for my budget; money was running out fast. The ferry left at 6 p.m. There were lots of bars and entertainment on board, so the time passed quickly. I arrived in London by means of ferry and train via Helsinki, Sweden and Denmark.

The End

THE BOAT PEOPLE

The storm ran around the village, vindictive in its fury, licking and flicking at the little huts until they folded and sank, sucked into the mud and rocks which tumbled and slid down the hillside, to be heaved and pushed and spat out onto the paddy fields below. The wind savaged the trees until the branches dipped and swung, stretching out to hug the wet soil. Mei fled through this waving green sea, wailing, hands fluttering and dancing in the air, thick strands of hair streaming like jet as her conical hat pirouetted into the gale.

As her bare feet directed her uncontrollable body on through the lashing jungle, down to the shore where wind and rain drove her to her knees, she sank groping, clawing, screaming at the sand to save her from the seething water, which took her, sucked her into its foam and left her encompassed in the infinite waste of the South China Sea.

Tran's boat, a small fishing vessel with a powerful engine and its desperate group of men and women, raced along the Vietnam Coast to escape the army patrol boat. Dodging into inlets, hauled around rocks, she burst into the swell of the fermenting sea knifing and slicing her way through a wall of mist. 'How provident the storm had been', Tran thought. 'Had they finally escaped?' He switched off the engine but could hear no sound except the slap and bump of the waves.

A bump!

'That was odd', he thought. Tran squatted and looked over the side of the boat. He grasped at an object in the sea only to find his fingers tangled in a black web. Mei felt an excruciating pain and her eyes slit open. She was being hauled unceremoniously up, up, legs jerking feebly in protest and dumped on a hard surface, where pale forms emerged, hovering and swimming above her. Spitting, heaving and sucking in air she rolled on to her side, too spent to be afraid. She heard voices muttering, 'She is half-dead, throw her back. We have not enough rice for another mouth.'

'Leave her alone' Tran glared at the occupants of the boat and turned to the wheelhouse. Mei shrank. Shocked and quivering, she dropped her head onto her knees and wept. She mourned for her lost parents, her younger brother and sister, entombed in mud and rocks. She had been a good daughter helping her mother cook and sew daily, after school, in the little thatched hut that had been home. Occasionally, before school, she had helped her father in the paddy fields planting and picking the rice. She had escaped the initial onslaught of the typhoon today – or was it yesterday?--because she had taken her father's place ploughing the land. Her father had stayed at home, his back bent and worn under the strain of ploughing the fields. Year after year he had trudged, silent and uncomplaining, back and forwards up and down behind the plough harnessed to the water buffalo shared amongst all the villagers, all now dead.

Mei wept for herself, old at seventeen, for her marriage arranged by her mother to a boy from the next village. It was to have taken place after Tet, the Vietnamese New Year, in the year of the dragon. Her mother had been proud of Mei's long silky hair and slim figure, her full lips and amber flecked black eyes. Her aquiline nose, a throwback from a French ancestor gave her pert face an unusual appeal.

Smearing her hand across her face to dissolve her useless tears, Mei timidly surveyed the group on the boat through a net of dripping black hair. Attired as they were in black baggy peasant trousers, loose tops and conical straw hats, she realised that they were refugees fleeing from the deprivation and torture that held all of South Vietnam in its grip, sending thousands of her countrymen to look for a better way of life away from the treacherous Viet Cong, the scourge of South Vietnam. Some escaped, others did not. Many were caught by the North Vietnamese patrols and taken to correction camps where they could remain, beaten and broken, for up to ten years, especially if they had fought for the Americans during the war from 1965 to the fall of Saigon in 1975. Pirates caught others; the women raped and left for dead, the men thrown to the sharks and the children taken prisoner. Many others drowned as their boats capsized in the deadly typhoons that swept through the South China Seas between the months of June and October.

This little boat to which they had entrusted their lives held four men, two women and two babies. Mei estimated their ages between 25 and 30, although they seemed older. She recognised Tran as the leader of the group and instinctively understood that her fate lay in his hands. Tran started the engine to slowly nurse his boat far out into the South China Sea where the mist released it like a butterfly emerging from its cocoon, the sun a golden disc in the sky. As night followed day, the little craft dipped to the froth and rose to the sun and stars. On to a new life with hope in their hearts, the refugees existed on congealed rice, fruit and rainwater.

One unforgettable mind-stretching night, the little band heard unfamiliar noises across the water. Breath held in fear, babies caught to the breast, dusky eyes piercing the darkness, they paused, frozen. 'Pirates', Tran breathed. The refugees threw themselves down on the deck, grovelling, sweating with apprehension – the only sound a stifled gasp. To Tran's ears the boat creaked with every wave as he watched the lights on the Thai pirate vessel lessen the distance between them. In the Cimmerian gloom a curious moan crawled across the water. Coarse laughter followed. Mei's instincts screeched within her to lie still, as her mind became a black abyss. Tran and his group bobbed silently out of sight and sound. The pirates were too engrossed to notice.

The fingers of daylight crept along the recumbent exhausted figures sprawled on the deck and with it came a strong sense of foreboding. Tran, his arm bent and locked stiff on the wheel uncoiled his lean body and stood listening. There was no sound from the engine. Going to the fuel tank he dipped a wooden chopstick in. It was dry. He looked around to see the others watching him. He shook his head. The refugees turned away to hide the anguish on their faces, eyes averted from each other. Hungry and thirsty the men and women squatted, lost in despair. Tran's eyes flicked over the group and his mind registered something else amiss. There was Vinh with her baby son and there was the other mother, Cuon. He searched her face as tears rolled slowly and silently from sunken sockets down sallow cheeks. 'When the pirates came, she started to cry and so I smothered her', Cuon whispered. She turned away, staring into the ocean depths.

The boat was now slapped and harried by the waves. They were drifting towards the Malaysian Coast according to the compass reading. Feeling helpless, Tran stood on the deck, arms folded, his black trouser legs flapping, his dark eyes slitted against the sun, the long lean length of him bowed into the breeze, frustration showing only in the twitch of his broad nose. Some time later he noticed a dark smear appear across the flat blue sky; he wondered if it was land. The others had seen it too. Suddenly hope vibrated in the air. The current carried them onward. Mei, her lithe young body, recovered from its ordeal, brushed Tran's arm. He looked down into smiling eyes and was happy that he had rescued her. She pointed excitedly out to sea where Tran saw a large, grey streamlined launch speeding across the waves towards them.

The refugees crowded around Tran in a group, sweat soaked faces grinning, conical hats nodding, hands flapping in hope and welcome. As they waited for the police launch to come alongside the sun glanced off a loud hailer held in a uniformed hand, which rasped its harsh message across the span of the South China Sea. 'You cannot land; Malaysia has over 50,000 Vietnamese refugees. We can take no more. Food, water and fuel will be provided and you will be towed out to sea for three miles.'

Hope splintered, extinguished abruptly. In vain, Tran pleaded with the officer. The men growled in helpless rage and the women sank silently to the deck, heads bowed. The baby slurped at his mother's breast. Irrespective of their feelings, provisions were put aboard, the engine repaired and the little craft pulled out to sea. The police launch stood off, to ensure that they did not return after dark.

Tran soon had the engine beating and sick with disillusionment, each in his separate misery, the little group of flotsam set off. Tran, tired and emotionally drained locked the wheel on course and slumping to the deck, fell into a disturbed sleep. Two hours later he was rudely awakened by water splashing on his face. A storm was brewing. If it was a typhoon he doubted they would survive. He shouted to the others to tie themselves to an immovable object and, holding the wheel steady, with the wrath of the wind behind them Tran steered the boat into the waves as it moved across the simmering surface in an effort to reach beyond the threatening storm. The light closed on a dappled sky, puffs of smoky cloud darting toward the horizon. Darkness, inevitable as time, settled on the hapless group. Mei came to stand sympathetically beside Tran.

Time became immeasurable. Rain lashed, wind and waves tore at the craft with its vulnerable cargo. Intertwined with misery was hunger as food and water were lost overboard in the boiling seas. Cuon too, had slipped overboard during the storm, nobody knew when and nobody saw her go. Perhaps it was a release.

Later the following afternoon, the battered storm-tossed vessel chugged slowly into sight of land. The refugees huddled uncomfortably; gazing in wonder, as the boat rode on, threading its way between a myriad of craft of all shapes colour and size, anchored or busy in the crowded waterway. Emerald hillsides peeped through a white mass as a string of soaring skyscrapers came into view brushing the lemon-yellow sky, each vying for the loftiest position on the verdant slopes. Tran remembered the quote of an ancient Chinese philosopher: 'And on that barren rock a million lights will glow.' This was

Hong Kong, unmistakable in its affluence and arrogance. The refugees sighed in unison.

With hope, that flaw of humanity flickering once more, they watched a large, grey, streamlined launch nose its authoritative way through the harbour towards them, the setting sun dancing off the loud hailer held by a uniformed hand.

The End

Lightning Source UK Ltd.
Milton Keynes UK
UKHW041258150719
346178UK00001B/4/P